Shadow Philoso and Cinema

M000194428

Shadow Philosophy: Plato's Cave and Cinema is an accessible and exciting new contribution to film-philosophy, which shows that to take film seriously is also to engage with the fundamental questions of philosophy. Nathan Andersen brings Stanley Kubrick's film *A Clockwork Orange* into philosophical conversation with Plato's *Republic*, comparing their contributions to themes such as the nature of experience and meaning, the character of justice, the contrast between appearance and reality, the importance of art, and the impact of images. At the heart of the book is a novel account of the analogy between Plato's allegory of the cave and cinema, developed in conjunction with a provocative interpretation of the most powerful image from *A Clockwork Orange*, in which the lead character is strapped to a chair and forced to watch violent films.

Whereas Plato compares the whole range of ordinary experience to shadows on the wall of a darkened cave, the author suggests that, in relation to cinema, audiences have the advantage that they know these shadows are not real. The result is that cinema more easily provokes the kinds of philosophical concerns it takes a special discipline to consider in relation to everyday life. This account of Plato's cave contrasts with the more usual reading, according to which images and art, and by implication cinema, only serve to bind their spectators more deeply to the shadows. Films like *A Clockwork Orange* demonstrate that while images can have a powerful impact on the attitudes of audiences, they also have the power to provoke them to critically examine their most basic assumptions.

Key features of the book include:

- A comprehensive bibliography of suggested readings on Plato, on film, on philosophy, and on the philosophy of film, aimed at readers who wish to pursue these themes further.
- A list of suggested films that can be explored following the approach in this book, including brief descriptions of each film, and suggestions regarding its philosophical implications.
- A glossary defining key terms from both philosophy and film studies that are mentioned or employed within the text.
- A summary of Plato's *Republic*, book by book, highlighting both dramatic context and subject matter, and functioning as a supplement to the book for readers who have not read this classical philosophical text in its entirety or who need a reminder of its scope.

Offering a close reading of the controversial classic film *A Clockwork Orange*, and an introductory account of the central themes of the philosophical classic *The Republic*, this book will be of interest to both scholars and students of philosophy and film, as well as to readers of Plato and fans of Stanley Kubrick.

Nathan Andersen teaches philosophy and film at Eckerd College, USA. He programs an award-winning cinema series in Tampa Bay, Florida, and is the co-director of the "Visions of Nature/Voices of Nature" Environmental Film Festival. He has published articles on the history of philosophy, environmental philosophy, and film.

Shadow Philosophy: Plato's Cave and Cinema

Nathan Andersen

Routledge
Taylor & Francis Group

LONDON AND NEW YORK

First published 2014
By Routledge
2 Park Square, Milton Park, Abingdon, Oxon, OX14 4RN

Simultaneously published in the USA and Canada
by Routledge
711 Third Ave., New York City, NY. 10017

Routledge is an imprint of the Taylor & Francis Group, an informa business

British Library Cataloguing in Publication Data
A catalogue record for this book is available from the British Library

Library of Congress Cataloging in Publication Data
Andersen, Nathan.
Shadow philosophy : Plato's cave and cinema /
Nathan Andersen. -- 1 [edition].
Includes bibliographical references and index.
1. Plato's cave (Allegory) 2. Clockwork orange (Motion picture) I. Title.
B398.C34A53 2014
320.092--dc23
2013040228

ISBN: 978-0-415-74205-4 (hbk)
ISBN: 978-0-415-74206-1 (pbk)
ISBN: 978-1-315-81490-2 (ebk)

Typeset in Sabon
by Taylor & Francis Books

Contents

Interpretation (epistemology)   126
Illuminating shadows (aesthetics)   128

Acknowledgments

Books don't write themselves; and no one writes a book by himself. Although only a few of their names appear within, this book could not have been written except after the works of so many others, who made films and wrote novels, or wrote on philosophy, film studies, or the philosophy of film. To name just a few, the most important and obvious: Plato, Aristotle, Immanuel Kant, Martin Heidegger and Maurice Merleau-Ponty, the three great Stanleys (Kubrick, Donen, and Cavell), Anthony Burgess, Malcolm McDowell, Gene Kelly, Hugo Münsterberg, Rudolf Arnheim, Siegfried Kracauer, André Bazin, V.F. Perkins, Laura Mulvey, Kaja Silverman, Gilles Deleuze, Allan Bloom, John Sallis, John Russon, Stephen Mulhall, Dan Shaw, Noël Carroll, Carl Plantinga, Michel Chion, Eyal Peretz, John Mullarkey, and Robert Sinnerbrink. Special thanks to so many who helped directly, through conversation and commentary on the topics discussed here during the percolating and planning stages, encouragement, editing and feedback on previous drafts: Jared Stark, Christina Petersen, Cathy Griggs, Jason Sears, Jim Goetsch, Andrew Chittick, Julie Empric, Ben Elliott, Paul Higgins, Aaron Garrett, Robert Sinnerbrink, John Mullarkey, Peter Costello, Kym Maclaren, David Ciavatta, Greg Recco, Susan Bredlau, Patricia Fagan, Ömer Aygün, Eric Sanday, Shannon Hoff, Kirsten Jacobson, Hunter Vaughan, Dan Shaw, and especially John Russon, for his mentoring and friendship for so many years, and for being an exemplar of the philosophical life. Thanks also to enthusiastic students in my film and philosophy classes through the years, especially Ryan Conrath. Thanks to Emma Joyes at Routledge, for her patience with me and enthusiasm for the project, and especially for saying yes! Thanks to Eckerd College for supporting the sabbatical leave during which the bulk of it was written, to the participants of the 2012 Toronto Summer Seminar on Plato's *Republic*, where I was able to talk about that astonishing book with lots of very smart people just as I was getting started, and for the Lloyd Chapin Faculty Fellowship that made it possible to be there and stay a few extra weeks in Toronto, sorting through the thoughts that followed. To Joel, Kate, Isaac, and Sorella – who thought it cool Dad was writing a book, even if I wouldn't let them see the film on which it was focused. Above all, and always, to Andrea.

Preface

A large group of prisoners sits, bound in the depths of an ancient cavern. Compelled forever to stare at shadows cast by a bonfire behind them, they consider these to be what's real. Mistaking appearances for true reality, only a few of them discover their error, when they're dragged from the cave and forced to see things by the blinding light of the sun. It's one of the most famous images from the history of philosophy, Plato's allegory of the cave, whose depiction of the condition of everyday life resembles nothing so much as the contemporary experience of watching movies. In fact, similar imagery is found and related themes explored in quite a number of relatively recent movies, especially science fiction films such as *The Matrix* or *Total Recall*, in which a leading character discovers that the world as he thought he knew it was a lie, an illusion. The ease with which the cinema depicts distortions of reality, giving weight to skeptical concerns that might seem abstract and unreal when described in the terminology of old books, has led a number of philosophers to become encouraged by the pedagogical merits of using film in the philosophy classroom.

Films naturally illustrate a wide range of philosophical issues, ranging from questions having to do with the conundrums of time travel, the relation between mind and body and the nature of personal identity, to ethical and aesthetic questions. In the past decade or so, a wide range of studies have appeared considering the scenarios presented in films and television programs as examples and illustrations of traditional philosophical themes. The approach to film that treats it as a source of illustrations and examples to introduce and explore philosophical themes – developed independently of reflections on cinema – has been described variously as "Film and Philosophy" or "Film as Illustration."

Yet films not only serve as handy illustrations of philosophical issues, but also raise philosophical questions of their own. Many of these questions overlap with questions of traditional aesthetics, applied here to a relatively new art form. What is film, and how does it work to communicate meanings? How is film distinct from other, more traditional, art forms and from newer ones such as multimedia, installation, and performance art? Do films have authors, and how does filmic narration differ from other forms of narration, such as those that operate in works of literature? For the past few decades, philosophers have begun to contribute approaches to film studies drawn from analytic philosophy and from traditional aesthetics. Other philosophers, inspired by cognitive science, have considered how we make sense of films, and what that can teach us about how the mind operates. "Philosophy of Film" treats film as an object of study, employing a range of philosophical methodologies to consider issues raised by cinema as a cultural artifact and object of experience.

Another approach, more influential for the present investigation, and more influenced by so-called "Continental" than "analytic" approaches to philosophy, has been labeled by many of its recent practitioners as "film-philosophy" because a central premise of the work is that film has something to contribute to philosophical thinking, and doesn't serve merely to illustrate philosophical themes or as a subject matter for aesthetic and cognitive investigations. Some have debated the question whether film can by itself be said to "do philosophy" – to pose and explore philosophical questions in ways that are distinctive and innovative as well as irreducible to philosophical approaches whose medium has traditionally been written and spoken discourse. Of course, even books don't "do philosophy" in the absence of readers to think and talk and write about the ideas therein – so a more fruitful line of inquiry into film's philosophical potential is to consider whether films contribute something distinctive to the ongoing discussions of philosophical questions, whether they provoke new thoughts and allow those who take them seriously to see and say things that hadn't occurred to them otherwise.

Proof of that can't be found by asking the abstract question whether it is even conceivable that films might generate philosophical insights incapable of being paraphrased in other ways. Issues are only confused if we require, further, that to accept a film as philosophical we need independent evidence that the director or writer intended it to be taken that way. The proof that film can contribute to the ongoing conversation that is philosophy is to be found in the proverbial pudding, in the actual experience of watching film and of specific films that provoke specific questions and generate distinctive insights. For those working in the tradition of "film-philosophy," the heart of their enterprise is rigorous film criticism – close "readings" and careful analyses of films and

cinematic conventions and of what makes them tick, with special attention to the meanings they generate, the concerns they raise, and the
insights they offer, overlapping with philosophical subject matters.

As a contribution to this approach, what I want to urge here is that
there are certain questions and concerns that are natural to cinema, in
the sense that thinking about film and about specific films can't help but
address these concerns. In my own opinion and to cite the words of
Stanley Cavell, one of the earliest and most influential contributors to
the "film-philosophy" approach, these questions are "matters internal to
what I think film is" (*Pursuits of Happiness*, p. 2). At the same time,
these questions, at the heart of any serious inquiry into film, overlap in
significant ways with some of the most basic concerns that have defined
the domain of philosophy for centuries: questions of reality and of the
relation between appearance and reality, which belong to the domain of
inquiry known as metaphysics; questions of interpretation and evidence,
central to epistemology or the investigation of knowledge and its limits;
questions of aesthetics, having to do with the nature of art and of film as
a distinctive art form; and questions of ethics, of choice and responsibility
and of the values at stake in action.

This way of approaching films – as artifacts that exhibit intelligence in
their design, and that naturally pose questions that are recognizably
philosophical – has the potential to bridge gaps between the range of
ways in which philosophers have approached film. Questions of aesthetics, central to the "philosophy of film", arise naturally in serious
discussions of cinema, which also means that considerations of specific
films have the potential to revise traditional thinking regarding aesthetics.
That means that here film is not merely an object of investigation, but
that films can "intervene" in such investigations, that films (or the
insights gleaned from their careful investigation) have the potential to
contribute to the conversations about them and about the aesthetic
categories employed to make sense of and reflect upon them. Likewise,
questions of "realism," as they surface in connection with specific films,
have the potential to contribute to our thinking what it means to say of
anything that it is real, or to clarify precisely the difference between
realities and their representations.

The approach to making sense of films here draws both upon the
vocabulary and analytical approaches of the film studies discipline and,
at a more basic level, upon the approach to making sense of anything
characteristic of the phenomenological tradition of philosophy. In particular, the approach here emphasizes the actual experience of watching
movies over the film itself, considered apart from an observer, or the
technical details of their production. Having said that, I make an effort

to avoid technical and philosophical jargon wherever possible and to explain concepts as they come up, whenever they are inevitable. While my thinking on all of these matters has developed over years of study and enjoyment of many films, works of film analysis, theory and criticism, and works of philosophy, both classic and contemporary, as well as through many conversations with students, colleagues, and friends, I avoid specific references except where I quote materials directly. This book is not intended primarily as a work of scholarship, whether in film studies, philosophy, or in the philosophy of film. It is aimed, rather, to outline and initiate an approach to thinking about movies in conversation with philosophy. Also, unlike many works along similar lines and from which I have learned a great deal, this one was written with the aim of being understandable to anyone with an interest in philosophy and film, and does not require any prior background in either film studies or philosophy. Readers are, of course, encouraged to watch the films discussed here and to follow up on references to other texts.

The broad approach to film and philosophy developed here draws specifically upon ideas and images developed in Plato's *Republic* – in particular the allegory of the cave and the criticisms of poetry and imitative arts – and upon insights and questions gleaned from a close study of Stanley Kubrick's *A Clockwork Orange*.

All quotations from Plato's *Republic* throughout the text are from the translation by Allan Bloom (Basic Books, 1991); page references are to the Stephanus pagination numbers.

Introduction

What we see on screen

To my way of thinking the creation of film was as if meant for philosophy – meant to reorient everything philosophy has said about reality and its representation, about art and imitation, about greatness and conventionality, about judgment and pleasure, about skepticism and transcendence, about language and expression.

(Stanley Cavell, *Contesting Tears*, p. xii)

On screen at the movies, we see people and things we recognize and understand. A man driving a fast car, his friends cheering behind him; a lighted sign in the driveway; a woman seated, reading in her house; a patient, in a hospital, or a hypodermic needle, inserted in a vial. They are the things of our lives, things we are familiar with from everyday life. Not always, of course. Some things we've never seen, whether because they go beyond the reach of our own experience, or because they don't exist at all, such as a monster or a time machine. We can accept and understand such things as part of the cinematic experience – at least as well as we understand many things in a world far too complex for us to understand much of anything – if they appear and behave as we expect they would if they happened to exist. Yet we know they don't – not only the monsters and time machines but the people and cars and hospitals and needles. They aren't there, not where we can get to them or interact with them in any way. There was, of course, at some point, a needle exposed to the camera, but it isn't that needle, the one that the doctor used to give that criminal the injection that would make him feel sick while watching violent movies, all as part of an experimental treatment in an unnamed country in a future not so different from our present. That needle, simply, does not exist. To enjoy the film, any film, is to rest easy with the paradox that we can say of something we see on screen what it is and who has it and how it got there, when we know it isn't really there at all.

To tell their stories, and explore their themes, filmmakers draw upon techniques and structures we recognize and understand. We know, for example, that a moving image of someone speaking followed by another image of another listening means the second one is listening to the first. We know that a close-up of someone's face needn't imply anyone has actually gotten closer, but that we are to pay attention to the expression or look on that face. Making sense of faces, considering what they communicate by way of an expression or a look, is something we do all the time, whether or not we're in the theater. The close-up draws upon and focuses deliberately a capacity we draw upon in everyday life. We can pick up on genre cues at the movies. We know when we're watching a Western or a science fiction film, and know that means we shouldn't be surprised if our hero travels through time. If that hero happens to be Bruce Willis, we know to expect he's a man of action and few words, we know to expect his thoughts and feelings to show in what he does and not so much on his face.

Some such devices, such as the use of stars, for communicating automatic meanings to the audience – what Stanley Cavell called the "automatisms" of film – are conventions that emerged in the history of cinema. Others are, we might say, phenomenological, in that they draw upon our capacities for making sense of the familiar phenomena of everyday life. They are part of what is involved in having experience at all, familiar to us by virtue of our inhabiting a common perceptual world with others, the world of everyday life. We draw upon them as for the most part we take them for granted, and yet when experiences trouble us or films call our interpretations into question, we often need to revisit the insights they communicate. A philosophical approach to film begins with an investigation of the ways movies communicate meanings, when we transform our automatic recognitions of significance into questions. Rather than exclaim, "Ah, there's a close-up! I know what that means!" we ask, "Just what is a close-up? Just what is *that* close-up? What does it mean?"

Yet an investigation of how we make sense of moving images is just the beginning. The meanings films communicate, the stories they tell, are rooted in the fact that we take for granted, as familiar and known, answers to a number of basic questions. Movies make sense and we make sense of them in much the same way as we make sense of anything – with some important differences having to do with the nature of the cinematic frame and other conventions of cinema – and yet they aren't just anything and we know they aren't real. To watch a movie is to see it as both like and unlike reality, or real life. To watch a movie, then, is to be operating with ideas of what is real and what isn't.

Questions about reality, about what it is and how it differs from appearances or images or simulations or representations, are questions that belong traditionally to the domain of philosophy. To explore the assumptions we operate with naturally when we watch films, to render such assumptions explicit, and to consider their implications, is to flirt with such philosophy.

Most films, whether fiction or documentary, are about people making decisions – decisions that can turn out well or badly for them, given what they want. Their story draws us in to the extent we care about their wants. We either want them to succeed or don't, which depends largely on whether we think they're right in wanting what they seem to want. This can mean merely that we like who they are and think what they want would be good for them, but it can also involve our assessment whether it is good for anyone to want what they want and act as they do. Of course films can and sometimes do lead us to care about and root for what we take to be the interests of characters we might in other contexts consider despicable. The issues here are complicated, and to begin to sort them out is to enter into ethical reasoning – yet another domain of thought that intersects with the interests of philosophy.

Nearly everyone has had the experience of watching a movie with someone else and then talking about it afterward, only to find they'd had a completely different experience. One loved it, the other hated it. One thought it a brilliant satire, exploring the hypocrisy of a culture that is liberally permissive and yet incapable of tolerating the consequences of its liberalism. Another thought it was misogynistic and hypocritical, glorifying the violence it pretends to condemn. Moviegoers and critics disagree not only on the aesthetic merits and ultimate meanings of films, but also on minor details of plot: what he meant when he said that to her, why they did that to him, whether this or that scene came before or after another, whether an event was real or fantasy or flashback. Moviegoing naturally raises questions of aesthetics and of interpretation and evidence. To pursue these questions is to enter the domain of philosophy; once again, to take movies seriously, to explore the questions films raise, is to do philosophy.

Films make sense to us, they relate to what we take to be real, they call for us to make aesthetic, epistemic, and ethical assessments. To pursue and examine the meanings films express and the questions they raise is to enter into considerations that relate directly to philosophy. Since these questions are not imposed upon but drawn from reflections on the experience of moviegoing generally and from the experience of immersion in particular films, they can be considered to define a domain of inquiry native to film. To pursue these questions is to engage in philosophy, but film's own philosophy. The insights gleaned from exploring film generally and specific films that highlight one or more philosophical concerns can and ought to be compared and brought into conversation with insights drawn from the literary tradition of philosophy, and yet there need be no presumption of priority here. The assumption that informs this study as a whole is that films – the hybrid products of technological mastery, business acumen (or stupidity), creative insight, and intelligence – are remarkable artifacts that often have a great deal to teach those who take them seriously. Films engage with and explore, in their own distinctive ways, the very same kinds of questions as interest philosophers, and philosophy has much to learn from cinema, at least as much as cinema studies can benefit when ideas and approaches from the tradition of philosophy are brought to bear on the fundamental questions about reality, knowledge, art, and ethics that films raise naturally.

To clarify how and why we might draw upon the insights and methods of the tradition of philosophy to investigate questions that arise naturally in reflections on film, what follows will examine and relate some of the central images and ideas of Stanley Kubrick's film *A Clockwork Orange* to themes from Plato's *Republic*. This may seem at first a strange pairing: a venerable and profound work of ancient Greek philosophy, whose central concern is with justice, and a highly stylized and controversial science fiction film depicting a violent city of the future, where hoodlums wreak havoc on the streets and the government exploits them for political gain. It turns out that despite their historical distance they share remarkable affinities in the range of the concerns they depict and examine.

In the *Republic*, Plato's teacher Socrates describes a utopia, an ideal city, in order to illustrate the interconnections between political and moral justice. Critical to the formation of both justice in the state and justice in the individual, as they appear in this work, is the establishment of educational reforms. *A Clockwork Orange* depicts a futuristic dystopia, a decadent state ruled by power-hungry hypocrites who are unable or unwilling to keep marauding gangs of carefree criminal youth from inflicting violence on the populace, at least until it starts to hurt them in the polls. The solution they hit upon, and with which they hope to score political points that will keep them in power, is a new approach to moral education, a technical solution to the problem of criminality. In *A Clockwork Orange*, technocrats promise a future in which criminals will be compelled to behave well; in the *Republic*, Socrates suggests the possibility of a city led by philosophers, who have insight into the true nature of the Good, and organize affairs such that citizens can best benefit the city by carrying out those activities to which they are most suited by nature and inclination.

Science fiction films often depict futuristic worlds that amplify features of the present, whose familiarity makes them feel contemporary, but whose exaggeration enables criticism and commentary on the contemporary reality. While in the *Republic* Socrates investigates the nature of justice by way of a thought experiment, *A Clockwork Orange* explores a corrupted future and by drawing upon audience intuitions regarding the role of government in regulating criminality encourages thoughts on the importance of freedom. Both works pose the question whether injustices are best addressed by means of punishment or reform. The *Republic* highlights interconnections between individual and political justice; *A Clockwork Orange* encourages audiences to consider the relation between individual freedom and political power. On the surface, at least, there are parallels between the central "message" of both the film and the dialogue, even if the ancient dialogue is more concerned with justice and the modern film more with freedom: Socrates aims to show that justice is intrinsically good even if it brings no outward benefits to the just person, and *A Clockwork Orange* suggests that freedom is valuable even if the free person behaves badly.

The *Republic* describes the role of music in shaping the moral character of youth; *A Clockwork Orange* depicts an apparent counterexample: a young man with a passion for classical music and an obsession for inflicting violence. The film likewise employs a soundtrack that for most audiences evokes feelings in contrast with those solicited by the actions it portrays. Its apparently casual misogyny, its depictions of violent gangs of youth, and of a corrupt government's response, led to the film being banned in Britain – which raises questions regarding censorship, a practice that Socrates himself apparently endorses when he suggests that poets and painters be banned from his ideal city. Both the film and the book provide occasion for consideration of the relative importance of reason and feeling, of philosophy and art in the formation of moral character.

It should be noted up front, however, that while it is a critically acclaimed work of a brilliant filmmaker at his creative peak, and in spite of its intriguing affinities with Plato's *Republic*, *A Clockwork Orange* is not an easy film to watch. It's an unsettling and violent film, even if its violence is highly stylized, rendered artistically and with a soundtrack designed to underplay, or at least complicate, the impact of its imagery. The film depicts rape, murder, and senseless brutality inflicted on helpless victims by aggressors who seem in it only for thrills. Even if it doesn't display actual forced intercourse – except when the lead character is himself forced to witness it on screen – and if it doesn't show audiences the bloody moment of death, as many films do now, their depiction in this film is unsurpassed for its visceral impact. Stanley Kubrick understood well that what is anticipated and left to the imagination can be far more horrifying than what is shown in all its gory detail. What is worse is the film's apparent misogyny – that the victims of the most violent acts are women, displayed throughout the film as sexualized objects, fully naked or only partially clothed, and often unwillingly disrobed. The young man who perpetrates its most violent acts is in fact the film's protagonist, whose point of view is largely shared by the audience, such that it is difficult not to feel at least a hint of his desire and fascination alongside our likely disgust.

Some say that it is just a movie, and violence is just one among many subjects that can be portrayed on screen. The point is entertainment, and we know it isn't real. One might defend the film on account of its aesthetic qualities – that the film deliberately stages its violent scenes in such a way as to make them feel like artistic performances, that the violence plays like dance, accompanied by music, as if the film were a sort of musical. Of course, it is just this tendency, to obscure violence and sexual objectification beneath a mask of high-minded civility, or in the form of high art, or mere entertainment, that the film seems to criticize – as its central figure employs the same civility, the same aesthetics, the same appeal to thrills, in order to perpetrate his own very real and unsettling violence.

What is more, while many films since have portrayed violence more realistically and explicitly, *A Clockwork Orange* captures powerfully the tension between the horror of the experience and the casual ease with which it can be inflicted. It depicts precisely the distance between real violence and active sexual objectification and their aesthetic counterparts, as these are found in art, advertisement, and propaganda, where they are designed to arouse desires that find satisfaction in consumerism or patriotic fervor, rather than to create social chaos when they are appropriated by impressionable youth. The film exaggerates, but it is not an exaggeration to say that images have impact, that they do shape feelings and aspirations. At the very least, the portrayal of violence on screen is appealing to young audiences, selling movie tickets and popcorn. Sex sells a range of products, and the objectification of women's bodies is an undeniable and ubiquitous aspect of modern media. *A Clockwork Orange* manages both to exploit the appeal of sex and violence, and to make it uncomfortable to watch, so that, like Alex during his treatment, we are both aroused and sickened. Because what we see on screen is seen to be at a distance from the everyday reality in which we take the appeal of more subtle forms of violence and objectification for granted, it enables a space for critical reflection upon the impact of that reality.

While in the *Republic* Socrates worries about the impact of stories and of images on the minds of those exposed to them, he at the same time creates one of the most memorable images in the history of literature and thought. He describes an immense cavern in which prisoners sit, gazing upon shadows cast by objects behind them, by the light of a bonfire. The shadows, he says, are what they take to be real, and we are just like them in our acceptance of appearances for truth. The allegory of the cave depicts human beings as enthralled to illusion, prisoners to prejudice. Only through philosophy, which involves the active investigation and testing of assumptions, can one be freed from these shackles. To escape from the cave, and free oneself from illusion, is to discover that the way things appear to us results ultimately from problematic assumptions we adopt regarding what is real, how we know it, what is good, beautiful, and worthy of pursuit.

This image of the cave bears a remarkable resemblance to the central image from *A Clockwork Orange* in which its central character, Alex, undergoes an experimental treatment designed to "cure" him of his criminal impulses. Seated in a theater and bound, with his eyes secured wide open, he is taught to associate feelings of sickness, medically induced, with images of mayhem that play out on the screen before him. It is a very different kind of education than the philosophical education proposed by Socrates, and yet the contrast and its failure are instructive. He is, according to the government, "impelled towards the good, by, paradoxically, being impelled towards evil." His antisocial instincts are turned against him, so that whenever he intends to act violently, he begins to feel deathly ill. He illustrates precisely a worry expressed by one of Socrates' interlocutors in the *Republic*: that just behavior is motivated by the fear of punishment rather than for its own sake. Socrates' response – that justice is its own reward, that being just amounts to having a healthy soul – is, paradoxically, illustrated by the ending of *A Clockwork Orange*, when Alex triumphantly pronounces he is cured of the cure, that he no longer feels sick contemplating violence. What can be seen in this so-called cure, powerfully displayed by the final sequence of images in the film, is an individual caught up in the extremities of self-deception. He isn't free, as he supposes, but a political pawn, who will prosper only so long as he remains useful to the current regime.

Plato's allegory of the cave has been frequently compared to the condition of audience members in thrall to a cinematic spectacle. Most such comparisons go no further than remarking on the resemblance. If they do consider where cinema stands in relation to the shadows that Plato compares to the world as it appears to us in the absence of philosophical insight, they tend to note that in relation to the movies we are somewhat worse than in a shadow realm. Movies, it might be thought, are copies of appearances, the shadows of shadows. In what follows I argue that we need to reconsider that relation, and suggest that, philosophically understood, the cinema is exactly on par with appearances. It belongs precisely to the shadow realm, but with a difference that amounts to an advantage for those who reflect upon it, that with respect to this shadow at least we know it is an appearance. When we see a man on screen we know he's not really there, that it is only an image. We forget – or don't know how to comprehend – the fact that according to Plato's allegory exactly the same thing is true of the man sitting next to us in the theater, that what we see of him and know of him when we think of him as simply out there, a thing among other things, is just a shadow of his being.

Comparing deliberately constructed moving images with appearances reminds us that appearances, too, are constructs. What we take ourselves to be encountering as simply out there, outside of us, is in fact the complex product of what we've gleaned based on haphazard and piece-meal encounters, put together imaginatively, based on prejudices and assumptions, some innate and some inherited or absorbed from our societies and cultures. Adopting a critical stance toward motion pictures, away from what simply appears and towards our ways of making sense of it, and exploring the assumptions and values we glean from them and bring to them, can help orient us similarly with respect to the broader realm of appearances.

Approaching cinema in this way is not merely a training ground for philosophy, but provides a space where real philosophy can and inevitably does take place, because to take films seriously and critically confronts us quite naturally with a range of basic and fundamental philosophical questions – questions of the relation between appearance and reality, questions of ethics, questions of knowledge and interpretation, questions of aesthetics. A critical approach to any film will, to some degree or other, engage with such questions, which is why it is no accident that filmmakers who take their discipline seriously are able (and others, perhaps, manage by accident) to find ways to confront and thematize some of these questions directly. Such films pose questions in a more intensified fashion, so that viewers are confronted with them upon even casual viewings. They might find that even to make sense of the plot is to pose such questions, or might find that these questions take on a felt urgency that merely academic queries tend to lack.

There are a number of ways this can happen, as when a film like *A Clockwork Orange* elicits our sympathies for an individual we also recognize to be morally reprehensible. A narcissist and sociopath, who cares only for his next thrill, Alex nevertheless wins admiration for his vitality and carefree charm. As wrong as we find his behavior, we can't help but find the state's solution to it repulsive as well, in its attempt to correct his violence by rendering him deathly nauseous at the thought of it. We can't help but see that acting in their own interests, and in their own way, albeit under protection of law, the state and its guardians can be as violent and arbitrary as Alex. Our conflicted response poses the question how justice is best served, whether it is worth pursuing at the cost of individual freedom, and whether the capacity to act upon urges even counts as a genuine expression of freedom. To follow up on such questions, and consider whether the film offers resources for responding, is as much an act of philosophy as it is the work of criticism. Good film criticism treats what is on screen as subject to investigation, something to ask about. It takes films seriously, exploring what they have to offer in the way of resolving the puzzles they pose. When the questions films provoke are philosophical, film criticism amounts to doing philosophy, and it can be done badly or well. To do it well is to follow up on the questions by taking cues from the film, and to put the answers it proposes into conversation with philosophical discourse beyond the film.

Because this approach to taking film seriously as a medium for philosophical reflection – incorporating philosophy within the shadow realm of Plato's cave – appears on the face of it to ignore or undermine Plato's critical assessment of the merits of imitative artworks in the *Republic*, in what follows we'll examine that assessment directly, and consider how some of the concerns he has raised there might begin to be addressed. Of course, young children, who lack the capacity to distinguish between moving images and reality, won't gain any insights into their condition as a captive audience from more exposure, and whatever philosophical insights might be gleaned from reflection on specific films may not vitiate the kinds of harmful effects Plato argues result from the easy gratifications they deliver to our basest impulses. The overall approach to film and philosophy is here illustrated and put into practice by way of a close analysis of the film *A Clockwork Orange*, a film that in its controversial reception highlights the contemporary relevance of concerns over the moral impact of movies.

1 Making sense of motion pictures

On faces and frames in Kubrick's
A Clockwork Orange

A face you won't easily forget appears on screen, centered, outlined sharply in the dark. It leans forward intently, so that a black bowler hat and hair below the ears frame the bright blue eyes that see you right through. It's a young man, with a crooked half-smile, welcoming but far from friendly, with long, sharp artificial lashes fixed upon the lids of his wicked right eye. Framed just to show his head and shoulders, wearing an open white button-up shirt and suspenders, he looks straight at you, motionless but for the rise and fall of his chest. Ready and alert, shoulders relaxed, with the poise of an animal prepared to pounce, his look is a challenge: see here, pay attention, hear me out, and as the frame opens slowly to take in more of his surroundings in what we'll learn is the Korova Milk Bar, he starts to speak. Rather, we hear a voice from no one's mouth but that can only be his. His lips don't move, as he raises up a glass of drug-laced milk to take a sip, but the voice's subtle blend of threat and invitation, its confident commanding tone, can only belong to that face, which now addresses us and begins to tell his tale.

So starts one of the most controversial films of all time, Stanley Kubrick's classic, *A Clockwork Orange*. The film still manages to shock for its aestheticization of sadistic violence, for its apparently casual depiction of misogyny and rape, and for making the vicious criminal at its heart its most seductive and sympathetic character. Considered by some both an indictment of youth anarchy and a critique of the politics that profits from its condemnation, it has also been held to glorify violence and to justify the contempt with which criminal youth often view the state. It was banned in Britain for a time due to reported cases of copycat crimes. Not only is it a thematic concern within the film whether life imitates art, and whether all forms of self-expression ought to be protected, but the very reception of the film intensifies these questions. On the one hand the film seems to champion freedom, against the intervention of the state, but on the other seems to offer a devastating critique of liberal tolerance. It is sometimes thought that the virtue of great works of art is to sustain multiple interpretations, that what makes them valuable is precisely that they generate argument and discussion. Before considering broader questions raised by this film, however, it is worth getting clear what occurs on its surface. What do we see and hear in the film, and in the opening sequences in particular, and how do the elements of the whole combine together to enable a cohesive experience that admits of competing interpretations and thereby poses serious questions?

Faces and frames

Films present us with image and sound. We see things – objects, places, people – moving about, doing things, and interacting. We understand what we see. For the most part, it makes sense to us. We know what the things we see on screen are, or at least what kind of things they are, and the kinds of things they do. We notice, or at least feel, the differences between different styles of camera movement. When moving images from different perspectives are joined together, one after another, we can usually tell when they're meant to suggest a sequence of events, when they're meant to suggest simultaneity, when they belong to different locations, or when they belong together as different perspectives on the same situation. Usually, the sounds we hear are easily linked to the images. We hear words and know who is speaking. We hear music and can read the cues to know whether it is something the characters hear as well, or whether it is music for our ears only, meant to accompany what we see, adding mood or rhythm. We make sense of what we hear and see. The specifics vary, but there are a range of repeating forms in cinema that are significant to us, both because we have grown up in a world that we've learned to make sense of and because a significant part of growing up in the modern world is to become familiar with moving images and their many variations.

The depiction of faces in film draws upon what we know from our everyday experience with faces, and amplifies and channels this knowledge by means of techniques and conventions of cinema. A close-up, in which just a face appears and fills up the cinematic frame, lets us witness, and sometimes share, emotions that go unspoken. A character's eyes, and our sense of where they are looking, help us to link images together, and make sense of the space they belong to. The "shot/reverse-shot" technique in cinema, for example, can show a face looking, and then cut to an image we identify as what that face can see. Voices we hear in the theater are linked to faces, and voices that we cannot link to the movements of a mouth on screen – usually known as "voiceovers" – can, but don't always, deliver a distinctive perspective on what we see, a narrative perspective that stands outside of what is shown. The camera, likewise, never appears on screen directly. It nevertheless defines a look, a way of facing the people and things that do appear, with which we may or may not identify. What the camera does show always appears within a frame, a window, as it were, that reveals varying perspectives without varying itself, in either size or location relative to us. Musical cues, and cues as to a film's genre, contribute to the mood in which the film is presented, and guide us in our path to making sense of the film, encouraging us to expect or accept the appearance of features of that genre. Some films bear the mark of a director, or of a producer or a writer, thereby suggesting a link between the various films to which that person or group contributed. Some films, also, make reference to themselves, or create images that suggest and encourage reflection upon the filmmaking process.

Face, image, cut, frame, movement, music, genre, perspective, narrative, voice, author, self-reference: these are some of the basic significant forms or meaningful dimensions that we take for granted in our encounters with cinema. What follows is a closer look at the opening sequences of *A Clockwork Orange*, that gives special attention to some of these most basic of the significant forms that cinema draws upon, and to the ways in which this film adapts familiar forms to the purpose of communicating specific thoughts and feelings. Careful attention to some of the significant forms of cinema and the ways they operate in the opening sequences of *A Clockwork Orange* provides a useful orientation into how this film provokes feelings and thoughts that challenge common-sense assumptions about how things are and ought to be.

Film's philosophy – the thinking that films can provoke about basic questions regarding what is real, what really matters, and how we make sense of it – is not a matter of hidden meanings, or of esoteric interpretations, except where the films themselves are esoteric, hiding clues to their significance. Films, for the most part, present us with stories – stories about people and things, about realities or possible realities that, generally, make sense to us, in more or less the same way as anything else does. We can say what happened, who did what and when and why. At the same time, like life, we do not always draw out or make explicit what is, on the face of it, obvious; and when we do we find that what appears to be obvious is just a familiar way of answering questions that could be answered other ways. Film's philosophy is what appears when we follow up on the questions that result from a careful attention to the meanings films present. Examining films closely, looking at what is there on screen and asking how it works, how it draws us to think and feel in the ways it does, has the effect of unsettling those thoughts and feelings. It has the effect of calling into question both the easy or obvious ways of making sense of the film and also, at the same time, unsettling easy and obvious assumptions about the kinds of realities the film depicts and that we also encounter outside the film. In some cases, at least, and clearly in the case of *A Clockwork Orange*, a careful look at the film will show it (or its makers) suggesting ways of thinking that resolve some of the questions its study provokes, directly or indirectly. At the very least, such films render problematic some of the more familiar or obvious answers to these questions.

First, to begin, a quick synopsis of this film. A charismatic young man, obsessed with Beethoven, skips reform school and spends his nights getting high, committing theft and acts of violence with his gang of young thugs. One night things get out of hand: he kills a woman and gets caught. Now in prison, his sentence is cut short after two years when he agrees to be the guinea pig for a new experimental treatment, a kind of aversion therapy in which he's drugged to feel horrendously sick while watching violent films. He can't now even contemplate harm without feeling wretched – and an unintended side effect is that Beethoven now sickens him too. After that he's powerless, a victim to his former victims, unable to fight back. Driven to attempt suicide, he becomes a poster boy for the opposition party, who aim to discredit the current government's flawed approach to crime. In the end, though, he's cured from the treatment, and resumes his former life in exchange for willingness to be used by that very government against the opposition.

Returning to the opening image, what do we see and hear? We see the face, the hat, the lashes, and darkness, framed. We hear the voice, narrating, giving name to face and place. What is it to see a face? To hear a voice? To encounter a frame? To see a face is not to see an object, what is merely out there, available to one's gaze, ready to be used and touched, assessed. To see a face is to witness the gaze of another. To see it is to see what sees, and to face a face is to see oneself seen. The surface of the face, the eyes, the lips, the brow and cheeks, shows, moreover, that the person we see is aware of being visible, aware of presenting a face, and is responsive to that fact. Muscles curl the lips into a smile or contort them to a grimace; eyes open up wide or narrow to a slit. Expressive, the face shows itself deliberately, sets the terms by which it is seen and encountered. In the face-to-face encounter, the face responds to another face by opening up, inviting its gaze, or closing off, rejecting it. Or it might show itself unaware of or indifferent to the other's gaze or presence. Faces, usually, share the same kinds of features, and roughly the same expressive capacities. The face of the other is equal to, and can mirror or refuse, or otherwise offer a responsive rejoinder to, the expression of the first. A warm smile, for instance, invites the other not merely to look but to share a look, to share a moment, to see eye to eye. The smile announces it is glad to see you, you're welcome in its presence, and asks for a smile in response.

What's with this half-smile, then, here in the opening shot? It can mean lots of things, as half-smiles do. It could be a facial tic, a muscle twitch, a genetic thing. It is hard to say right away without seeing more, and to take it as a hint of sinister might just be to get it wrong. It is not, though, an isolated malice: it's in the eyes, it's in the incongruent lashes, in the way he knows to tilt his head so the rim of his hat just obscures his forehead, and accentuates the look. Still, it could be just a pose, and we can't be sure just yet. A face can mask as much as reveal its attitudes on what sees it and what it sees.

To see a face is to see what sees, but also to encounter limits to vision. I see that the other sees, but what she sees I can't be sure, even if I follow her gaze; how she sees it, and what she thinks about it, I can't tell. She has to speak. She has to tell me. A clear picture of her perspective can emerge only through words. Then again, words, like faces, can deceive as much as reveal. More about words later, when we consider these words, the words that emerge with the same half-smile we encounter on this face.

If to face a face is to see oneself seen, we don't face this one. It isn't, quite, a face. We see it; it can't see us, at least not specifically. We may feel the hint of menace, may feel ourselves seen, but know that we are not. He can't touch us, and we can't touch him. He's not here where we are, but somewhere else, a space we witness but cannot share. A sequence from later in the film, set in the same bar, shows what it would be really to encounter that face, that look, that same inviting threat.

Following a wild night inciting and inflicting violence, the young man, Alex, and his gang – "droogs," he calls them – return to the Korova Milk Bar to relax. Across the way a group of older, well-dressed folk chat casually, when the jukebox stops and the woman among them sings a lovely bit from Beethoven's Ninth, the "Ode to Joy." Alex listens, entranced, until the droog he calls Dim lets out an interrupting belch. Alex canes him fiercely across the leg, and Dim protests, upset. An argument ensues but not before Alex tilts his head to the woman, a smile like the one we've seen already, but with possibly more warmth. The woman watches him across the way, wary and concerned, unsure how to take his appreciative toast and nod. There's real threat there, real worry in her eyes. She sees what we see, a dangerous hoodlum, a situation that could erupt in violence. We see the same, we feel its danger, but as we're not a part of the situation there depicted, we don't have to react. We can't. We can close our eyes, walk away, but we are otherwise unable to affect what we see. We don't face that face, only its moving image, framed.

To call it a moving image, though, can be misleading. I see my own image in a mirror, in a photograph, or in a drawing by my daughter, and when I do I consider the resemblance. Whether they are created naturally in a mirror or deliberately in a painting, we tend to think of images as copies or representations, bearing some likeness to that of which they are the image. Here, though, what we get in the opening frame is just Alex, with his enigmatic half-smile and bowler hat. It is not a copy, because he isn't elsewhere, except perhaps in the pages of a book by Anthony Burgess on which the film is based. We can say it is an image of young Malcolm McDowell, all dressed up to look like Alex, but when the movie was released, at least, McDowell was largely unknown, and the film all the more effective for it. Plus, to focus on that is to lose track of the movie, to break out of its spell, as when we can't see past a big-name actor to the role he inhabits. Caught up in the experience, we forget about all that, or are at least able to set it aside, except insofar as a familiarity with the actor's star persona is relied upon or manages in any case to shape our sense of who he is here.

If we like, we can still call it an image, if only to emphasize that to grasp it requires imagination. To be an image at all, it must be both sensed and imagined; there are no images in complete darkness, or in the absence of someone to entertain them and make sense of them. The whole that is the film, moreover, hangs together because we hold it together, imaginatively. At each moment, we might say, we see only a passing picture frame. Without some continuity, without some link to what came before, it would be only a passing blip, we'd be lucky to notice at all. We link images together, we hold on to the past and see this image continuing the last, anticipating developments in the next. This is true not only of the visuals but also of the sounds and intimations of other sense modalities that all form part of the filmic experience. We link images and sounds together based on cues to construct an imaginative whole, in an attempt to make sense of it all. If this image is an image of someone, and the voice belongs to anyone, it is to Alex, who exists by virtue of belonging to the world of the story imagined and written down by Anthony Burgess and modified for depiction on film by Stanley Kubrick. Assuming, that is, these are the same world, and the same Alex, it is a world we can only access by making sense of those words, imagining these images. We can entertain it, but we're not and can't be part of it; it stands apart.

Consider how we make sense of this sequence of images: the opera singer looking, concern in her eyes, alarm creasing her mouth; Alex raises a glass, tilting his head with a cocky smile. We never see an image showing both Alex and the singer together in the same frame, let alone facing one another. We do see, previously, the woman in a wider shot with friends, surrounded by naked white mannequins like the ones surrounding Alex and his droogs. We might assume, on that basis, they're in the same bar. These two images, though, read more specifically than that: the singer looks *at* Alex and friends as he raises his glass *to her*. We see her worried look. We see his self-confident gaze. We read: they're in the same room and looking at each other. To see a face is to see what sees, but not what it sees. The face's image, then, is incomplete. It poses a question: what does it see? To face the face is to have an answer: she sees me. Otherwise we must look elsewhere for the answer the film supplies here through its sequence.

We sometimes call the sequencing of discontinuous images a "cut," so named for the fact that before the rise of non-linear computer-based editing it used to require the actual slicing of celluloid strips. It might be better to call it a "linkage" (or use the French term, *montage*) since its effect is to bring images together, requiring audiences to make sense of the joining. Here we see a face, looking, and then another face, looking. The images are, on their own, incomplete, and the act of imagination, which follows up on cues delivered in the cut, places them together in the same room, looking at one another, answers the question, completes the picture.

These images, all of them, even those we construe as occupying distinct imaginative spaces, appear in the same location relative to us. They all fit the same frame, in front of our eyes, the same projected rectangle, shaped of light and shadows. We call them "moving images," because what we see inside the frame is constantly changing. Sometimes objects or people on screen appear to move with respect to the frame; sometimes it seems that the frame itself moves, changing perspective on what is there on screen. With respect to us, though, the frame remains the same rectangle, in the same place, there before us on the TV set or on the movie screen. Its borders and function remain the same as the images within are changing.

To frame is to enclose. The frame establishes a border, setting what is inside apart from what is not. The motion picture frame frames in at least two ways. It marks the perimeter of the entire moving image, in distinction to extra-filmic realities. Usually, we see more than what is there, contained within the frame: the unilluminated portions of the screen, the theater wall or television enclosure, the chairs and other people's heads in front or seated nearby. The frame signals these as outside of the film, marks them off as inessential, and to pay attention to the film is to pay them little mind. On occasion, though, the film references what is outside of the frame, by calling attention, at least, to the fact that it is a film, and that there is an audience watching it – as in the opening image of this film when Alex looks at us and addresses us directly.

Equally important, the frame marks limits to the current image, as distinct from what it might show later. The opening, for example, is framed tightly, revealing just Alex's head and shoulders – what is called a "close-up" – and later widens, showing more of the bar. Given what we know of how things are before we enter the theater, we expect there's a body below that head, just as we expect that body has a back side we might see later, and expect there is a room in which he's seated. At any given moment, though, the frame reveals only a selection of the filmic reality we anticipate or imagine based on what we've seen so far. The current selection offers a perspective on that reality, and changes in the image resemble changing perspectives upon it: moving closer or further, turning left to right, up or down. Discontinuous shifts or cuts, as from Alex to the singer, offer differing perspectives. We need to piece them together to make sense of the whole. They form axes, as it were, from which to organize the shape of the imagined space.

While images within the frame offer perspectives we can share, we don't quite inhabit them. We remain outside the frame, in the sense of being entirely outside the moving image and all that the frame can and will reveal. There is a difference between our perspective, seated in a theater or on a couch looking at the frame, and the window it offers up into the space it depicts. The overall shape of that space, though imagined, isn't arbitrary. The perspectives are themselves fixed by the frame, and don't change based on who's looking or where they sit in the theater. We don't always take it all in, as we focus on this or that detail. We can and can't help but be selective in our attention to the details revealed by the frame's current orientation, but we can't modify that orientation by ourselves. It is what it is, for everyone in the audience, no matter how each happens to be situated with respect to the screen. We can turn our heads and squint our eyes to narrow in on specific details, but we can't look around things (even if the film we're watching is so-called 3D), and to turn our heads too far is to turn away from the frame. We don't inhabit these perspectives, and can't actively shape them. We can only witness and make sense of them.

The film, then, offers up multiple moving perspectives, distinct from our own, that nevertheless solicit our capacity to piece them together. Students of cinema often speak of these moving perspectives using vocabulary drawn from the production of film, referring to camera movements or techniques such as "panning" or "tilting" or "zooming" or "tracking" or "dolly-shot." It is important, though, to note what difference these make to the experience of cinema, to the ways audiences make sense of what they see. At that point the camera and crew have done their job, and are out of the room, and we're left making sense of images in their absence. What matters, then, is not what the camera did but how this impacts the sense of the image within the frame.

Take, for example, the opening shot. It starts out tightly framed on Alex's face and then opens up to include the whole space, the Korova

Milk Bar. We see Alex, staring intently, and then his face remains centered as the frame opens slowly to include his droogs, Dim and Georgie and Pete, who are posed, unmoving, almost like statues. The frame opens wider to reveal the naked mannequins arranged erotically as furniture and appliances throughout the room. The slow and smooth opening of the frame could be achieved technically in at least two different ways: by moving the camera backwards, away from Alex, on a dolly track to keep it smooth, or by starting zoomed in with a telephoto lens and then zooming out slowly. It makes a difference, though, which method is selected. In the first case, as the camera pulled away from Alex, there would be a continuous shift in the spatial relationships between him and what surrounds him. As the camera pulled away from the central figure, for example, objects initially obscured by this figure would then come into view. This looks natural, because it is just what happens when we move away from a nearby object. In the second case, as the camera zooms out it is simply including more in the frame, without changing relative positions at all. The initial close-up appears, in hindsight, to have been merely a narrow selection from a given wide perspective.

This looks more artificial, and suggests an act of selective attention rather than an actual movement. A contrast with this approach can be seen in a later Stanley Kubrick film, *The Shining*, in which he pioneered the use of the Steadicam to achieve stable moving perspective shots throughout the Overlook Hotel, notably traversing its topiary labyrinth, covered in snow, as Jack chases his son Danny. This kind of shot, achieved smoothly by the use of special stabilizing equipment or with a dolly on a track, resembles the movement of a perceiver through space. The zoom shot, by contrast, suggests an initial narrowing, selection, or focus, that then opens up to establish its setting. In this case, and several other instances throughout the film, Kubrick's team chose the latter, starting out narrow on Alex's face, then zooming out slowly to include all of the room. The approach privileges in significance what is there in the initial frame, only afterwards setting it in a larger context. This also contrasts with a more usual method of scene editing, which provides first an "establishing shot" and then employs a series of medium-range and close-up shots to place the action of the scene within its setting.

An additional effect of this zoom shot, felt in hindsight as the image widens without a change in proximity, is to focus attention on Alex's face but from far away, revealing that even in the close-up we remained at a distance. His face fills the frame, but we never get close. It is framed tightly, but not quite "close-up." A similar effect is achieved in the cut we considered above, from a zoomed-in shot of the opera singer to a wider shot of Alex. There is, at one previous point, another tight shot of Alex's face watching her, to show his blissful appreciation of her singing, but at that point she's apparently unaware of Alex. When they look at each other, he appears in context, with his gang, now rebellious, seated nearby. The two framings establish they're looking at each other, and the tight frame on the singer lets us see clearly the concern on her face, but without eliminating the distance between her and Alex, or giving any hint of intimacy to their face-to-face encounter. He looks at her, ignoring her friends. She looks at him, and sees his dangerous gang. Likewise, the effect of the zoom in the opening shot is to emphasize what we've already noted regarding the initial image: that this face commands attention, without in any way mitigating the danger or distance. We see its expression, and remain far away.

Style, music, and voice

A very different proximity appears in the film when, to culminate their evening's entertainment, Alex and friends decide to pay a surprise visit to a home outside the city. They arrive late at night after a dangerous joy-ride in a stolen car. We see them creeping up slowly in the dark, past a sign reading "Home," to a large modern house, surrounded by trees. The

frame cuts inside, to a balding man in pajamas, typing at his desk, a large bookshelf behind him. We hear the doorbell ring and he looks to his left, wondering aloud who it might be. The frame follows his look and tracks to our right to reveal a woman, his wife, in a red jumpsuit, seated, reading in an egg-shaped enclosure. She'll see who it is, she says, and walks up two short flights of stairs to a mirrored hallway, when the image shifts to show her making way to the door. The smooth perpendicular movement, composed symmetrical framings, and simple cut here serve to expand our sense of the shape of the place, without in any way suggesting a subjective point of view, such as a turning head or locatable gaze. This is in stark contrast with a number of images that follow.

As soon as Alex and gang have entered the house, dragging the woman along as they traipse through the hall, the image becomes much more kinetic. This is now clearly a handheld shot, that sways and bobs slightly from the main room's upper level as it tracks the hoodlums' entrance, leaps down stairways and over the bannister, as Alex plants a flying kick to the face of the writer, who by then had left his room and climbed the stairs to investigate. The man somersaults backward and George leaps upon him, pinning him down, as Dim twirls around laughing with the woman over his shoulder and Pete jumps on the couch, as Alex calls all to order. Gone are the smooth movements and symmetrical framings. It's handheld shaking and extreme distorted close-ups from now on. Apart, that is, from when Alex begins his song and dance, kicking the writer half-conscious and cutting the jumpsuit from the woman to the tune of "Singin' in the Rain," as he prepares to rape

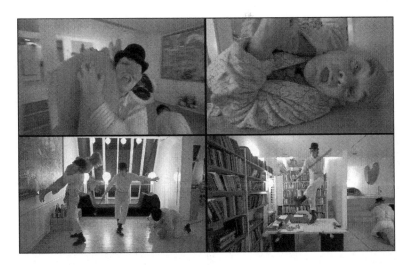

her in front of the terrified eyes of her husband. Shots of Alex singing and striking, leaping up on the desk and knocking over the bookshelf, are, once again, all wide, open, smooth, and symmetrical.

Consider the impact of these differences. There are, of course, technical differences: hand held, shakes, and blurs, versus steady, stable cameras on mounts. The wide-angle lens for the close-ups adds a bit of "fisheye" distortion to faces nearby; contrast that with the undistorted tight frame of the opening shot, achieved by telephoto lens. The effect of the difference is to accentuate the visceral, the real fear and experienced violence. Alex's dance feels staged within the stable frame. He considers himself something of an artist of violence, a performer, who sets his exploits to a soundtrack in his head, which in this case he belts out for all (and us) to hear. In a previous scene from the same evening, they'd run into another gang that was ripping the clothes off a struggling young woman. They were, then, literally on a stage as Alex and the rest observed and approached from below, interrupting and challenging them to a brawl. One gets the sense even then that, far from being bothered at all by the rape about to take place, and apart from his general enthusiasm for any kind of fight, what Alex objected to was the staging of their act, its bad choreography. They're talentless hacks. They're in it only for kicks. Alex wants admiration and applause, and we are his captive audience. The shaking camera and distorted close-ups of the next scene, however, undermine his aesthetics; they highlight the contrast between his improvised choreography and the reality of its victims. What we see in this scene alternates between, on the one hand, an apparently impartial, objective, but aestheticizing viewpoint which suggests the theatricality of the violence as at least Alex construes it, and, on the other, the more frenetic and subjective close-ups on the faces of the victims, which show their genuine sense of horror at what takes place and befalls them.

The way in which these images are constructed pushes the audience to differentiate between the rape as it is experienced by the victim and her husband, the writer, on the one hand, and Alex and his droogs, on the other. Depicting a difference in the way it is experienced provokes us, also, to consider the difference between depictions and the event itself, between the reality of the rape and the way in which it is felt and interpreted by its participants. There is, additionally, a difference between the two perspectives and how we, as an audience, experience their depictions. How we experience it depends, to some degree, on our own personal experiences and cultural background, our assumptions about gender, and our attitudes towards violence, and these are also shaped by the history of our interactions with depictions of rape and violence in the media. Experience is never merely a matter of something happening, to which we react as passive spectators. We are always involved and affected in some way or other by what goes on around us, and it always involves us in the activity of making sense, and we make sense of things based largely on the specific history of our various prior encounters. Certainly, Alex's sense of what he is doing is shaped by his own past, including his experience watching other motion pictures, such as *Singin' in the Rain*. By contrast, while both the writer and his wife were wary, and obviously aware of the possibility of danger as they opened their door to Alex, they were nevertheless clearly unprepared for the violence and violation of the sudden encounter that came to utterly overwhelm their senses.

Real terror hits home. There's no aesthetic distance, no symmetry, no wonder, no play, and no stage. It is right there, in your face, everywhere you look. At home, before the arrival of the violence, the writer and his wife – Mr and Mrs Alexander, as they're named in the novel and the credits – sit relaxed, calm, at ease. Separated by a partial wall, they nevertheless appear to feel not at all alone. She strides to the door, calmly, despite the unusual hour. She voices hesitant concerns about letting in strangers, but, after all, it was their home, a place of safety, and they're good people, they help those in need. Hearing Alex's pretense of a nasty accident outside, the writer shrugs calmly, "I guess we'd better let them in," and the woman apologizes for her understandable reluctance as she unlatches the door. From that point on, though, they have no stable point of reference, their vision's come unhinged. Their home is violated. Alex is at ease, but what they see is chaos, and what we see close-up is the horror in their eyes. The look on their faces is not the gaze of mastery they'd exhibited at home while relaxed, or even the composed look of concern we witnessed on the face of the singer, who felt largely protected by her friends and the public setting. They don't ever quite face Alex, who in any case is wearing a mask, a phallic nose protruding just below his eyes. They don't see eye to eye with anyone, but stare frantically, uncomprehending and helpless in the face of this traumatic violation.

But Alex wants a witness. He insists upon it. First, though, he silences his victims, placing large rubber balls inside their mouths, secured with packing tape. It's all done with flair, as far as he's concerned: with a slide to the side, he unrolls the tape wide. Then he wraps it secure around their heads to the rhythm, apparently oblivious to the fact that instead of an orchestra he's accompanied by the maniacal, giddy laughter of Dim and the others. We see, though, how it looks to the writer, helpless and writhing, with a bloodied mouth, as George finishes the job. After knocking over the bookshelf, Alex returns with a pair of scissors to slice through the woman's garb. At this point, instead of seeing things straight on as from a stage, we occupy a position from below, just behind the writer's head. The frame now alternates between this per-spective, one directly facing the writer's horrified face, and a third showing the woman, her terrified eyes, muted and helpless in the strong grip of big Dim.

Alex finishes the song and dance right after he drops his pants. He leaps down to the floor and puts his long, fake nose right into the face of the writer, admonishing him in nadsat slang (which Burgess tailored for the novel) to look on as his wife is raped. "Viddy well, little brother. Viddy well," he says. It is worth recalling that Alex as narrator addresses us the same way, calling us his little brothers, and his only friends, as he invites us to witness his life and crimes. It might appear as if the writer could not do otherwise than watch his wife's assault, given that he is pinned down, his face secured in her direction. He does blink, several times, suggesting that he'd like to close his eyes, but seems to open them wider each time, as if there's something in him that insists on being witness. A close-up shot, as Alex leans down before him, shows Alex's phallic nose pointing right towards his eyes, as if the demand that he look on is a kind of rape of the writer's face, an assault upon his eye-balls. It is hard not to think that something like that is happening to us as well, except that we can turn away. We also, if we continue to allow the film to work upon us, hold our eyes wide open, even as we're hor-rified and as much as we might consider that we ought to look away or leave. We're not pinned down, though: we're in the theater by choice. We are interested, gripped.

Alex narrates the film, encourages us to see things from his point of view and to care about what happens to him. He is, to begin with, pro-tagonist. What's more, from the opening shot, and as Alex introduces himself, he becomes something of a fascination. His words invite us in and seduce at the same time as they intimidate. He adopts a tone throughout that presumes sympathy with his aims and desires. He introduces us to himself and his three droogs, and to the Korova Milk Bar and the "milk plus" that it sells, which they drank to sharpen up for bouts of what he calls "the old ultraviolence." At that point we shift to a new setting: an aging hand in a worn-out jacket holds a bottle half-full, with an empty one beside and bits of garbage strewn about. The shot slowly zooms back, as in the opening shot, to show an old man, a bum, reclining on the concrete, drunk. He sings an old Irish ditty, about "Molly Malone," and as the frame reaches its widest point, his body is intersected by the long shadows of four men. At that point Alex begins to narrate again, telling us how much he dislikes seeing such things. "One thing I could never stand, is to see a filthy dirty old drunky" – and the camera cuts now to a shot of Alex and friends, approaching the old man slowly. At that point, we might imagine, they're on a misguided mission, to clean up the streets, to do what police and politicians can't to right the wrongs of a broken society. As shocked as we may well be by their ultimate methods, he could at this point just seem mistaken, in need of new direction. It's like they're playing cops, cleaning up the streets, enlisting unwitting strangers as the element to overcome. The next scene, as well, leaves a similar impression. They stop a rape in progress by a rival gang, as mentioned already, and then manage to incapacitate the perpetrators, until the real police arrive on scene. At that point we might think Alex has generally right instincts, aimed at preserving what is good and eliminating the evils of a society gone wrong, only takes it too far, and into his own hands. We can think all that, or along those lines, and Alex's words suggest it, until we reach the scene of rape in the home of the writer. At that point his perception of himself as sympathetic, and our possible perception of him as a misguided protagonist, is severely unhinged from the reality of his actions.

How Alex sees himself, and how he sees his actions, is communicated to us not only by his words, but also by the music accompanying his various exploits. If the incongruity of word and action is a recurrent theme throughout the film, it is the felt incongruity between situation and soundtrack that's most blatant throughout. Alex attacks and murders to Rossini, masturbates and dreams of assisting in a crucifixion to the sounds of the "lovely lovely Ludwig Van" (Beethoven). Nowhere, though, is the tension clearer than in the scene of unprovoked assault and rape in the home of the writer and his wife. After barging into the house, with the writer held down by Georgie and his wife held up by Dim, Alex breaks into song and an improvised dance around the helpless couple, punctuating each sentence with a punch or a kick or a smack with his cane. The song he sings is "Singin' in the Rain," the most memorable and joyous tune from the classic musical of the same name. In that film Don Lockwood (Gene Kelly) walks home in the dark through a downpour, exuberant after a momentous meeting, in which he both solidified a budding relationship with the woman he loved and discovered how to salvage his motion picture career from an impending flop. The camera anticipates his every unexpected move as he taps and leaps and kicks his way over obstacles, around confused and hurried passersby, and through the wet streets, singing enthusiastically of his renewed self-confidence and unabashed love. The lyrics of the song itself embrace an incongruity: that what should be a downer (a walk through a downpour) only elevates his spirits. They seem nevertheless an awful fit for the horror of a home invasion.

We'd already encountered, though, the music of Rossini playing as soundtrack to the slapstick viciousness of the brawl between Alex's gang and that of his rival, Billy Boy. Later we'll hear Beethoven as score to even more heinous images and acts of ultraviolence. That Alex has the poor taste to sing a joyful song as he inflicts pain is hardly the worst of his vices. The music manages at once to aestheticize the horror of the situation, turning its real and felt brutality into just another musical number, and at the same time it accentuates it, exhibiting Alex's callous lack of concern for the suffering of others. Its specific use here also serves to deliver a number of interconnected insights into the connection between sound and image, and between words and action, in cinema and in life. The lessons are clearest if we recall something else about the appearance of this song in its original context that makes it peculiarly appropriate for appropriation here.

In *Singin' in the Rain*, Gene Kelly plays Don Lockwood, a silent film star who publicly pretends to be romantic with leading lady Lina Lamont (Jean Hagin), but is actually in love with Kathy Selden (Debbie Reynolds), who initially pretends to find him insufferable. Following the commercial success of "talkie" film *The Jazz Singer*, his studio's head decides to add sound to their latest picture. The problem is that for all her quiet loveliness Lina Lamont sounds just awful, and a test screening makes clear that the picture will flop. Don's best friend Cosmo (Donald O'Connor) and Kathy try to cheer him up, and they hit upon the bright idea of turning their film *The Dueling Cavalier* into *The Dancing Cavalier* and making it a musical. He loves the idea, and they celebrate with a playful song and dance throughout the house to welcome in the morning, at the end of which it hits him: Lina can't sing and she can't dance and there's no way she can be part of a musical. That is, until Cosmo has another bright idea, inspired by a moment during the test screening when the soundtrack slipped, and Lina's face was mouthing the male villain's lines. Cosmo's idea, which he illustrates by having Kathy sing behind him as he moves his lips to the same tune, is to have Kathy do the speaking and singing while Lina lip synchs, for just this one picture, to make it a success.

Don takes Kathy home in a taxi, which waits as he kisses her in the doorway. She remarks on the unfortunate torrent, and looking her straight in the eyes, he proclaims, in all sincerity, "from where I stand the sun is shining all over the place." He waves the taxi off and walks home smiling in the downpour, closes his umbrella, and begins to sing. "I'm singin' in the rain, just singin' in the rain. What a glorious feeling, I'm happy again. I'm laughing at clouds, so dark up above. The sun's in my heart, and I'm ready for love." Why does Alex choose just this song as soundtrack to their violent act? It is not raining when they arrive at the home – although it is raining later when Alex returns to the writer's home by accident, following his aversion therapy treatment. An easy answer might be that, as we learn, Alex loves music, and this is the song that came to mind. He will, later on, tell the scientist preparing him for treatment that he does "like to viddy the old films now and then." He must have seen this one and was struck by its style. He might also like the irony, that his own delight in "ultraviolence" outweighs (for him) the gloom of their suffering. That is, of course, a perverse interpretation of the overall theme of the song – that external events needn't determine one's mood – since in this case he is clearly the rain and they're clearly not singing. That might be enough to account for things from his twisted perspective, but doesn't explain the filmmakers' choice (the song doesn't appear in Burgess's novel) and doesn't account for the impact of the song here on those who know and love the original film.

First, the fact that the original film is a musical suggests an assessment of this scene, and, perhaps, of the film as a whole, in relation to the musical genre. Musicals can be more or less realistic overall, but what they ask us to accept is that characters who might otherwise behave plausibly might nevertheless, unexpectedly, express their feelings and ideas through spontaneous song and dance. Sometimes there's a semi-plausible rationale for the musical numbers, as in *Singin' in the Rain*, where the lead characters sing and dance and write music for a living. That's not always so, though, and even here it defies credibility to think they'd hit upon such inventive and elaborate lyrics and routines off the cuff and on the fly. That means that for a musical to work, the audience has to embrace the convention that the musical numbers needn't be realistic, and accept them for their capacity to entertain and to express something about the characters, their feelings, and their situation, through song and through dance.

There is often a dreamlike dimension to musical numbers in film. They seem as if they're set apart from the main line of the narrative. They communicate a great deal about how characters feel or what they are doing, but in ways that aren't strictly like life. A musical number can collapse time, give a sense for a sequence of events taking place over a lengthy period but presented in the course of a single song. Even movies that aren't strictly musicals, such as *Rocky* and *Karate Kid*, exploit the power of music to express a long passage of time spent training as if it were all a compact dream. Musical numbers often also, like dreams, allow characters to clarify and express feelings they aren't prepared yet to admit. Characters might sing to one another words they needn't be thought to have said, words that give voice to what, perhaps, may have been the expressive content of only a few passing glances. Such musical numbers, like dream presentations and flashbacks in film, solicit audiences to make sense of them differently than they would more usual sequences.

Piecing shots together, we've seen, is the work of active imagination, which retains, anticipates, and links images, making sense of them as perspectives that somehow fit together into a coherent sequence in space and time. Even there, where some images are clearly presented from a narrow or biased point of view, overall coherence is never more than partial and open to revision. Flashbacks can be tricky. They suggest that something's happened, but can feel like subjective memories of events rather than reliable depictions. This is even more the case when images are implied to be fantasies or dreams – as happens several times in *A Clockwork Orange*, when Alex's face takes on a look of orgiastic bliss and we witness his vampiric fantasies of power and destruction accompanied by Beethoven. Likewise, while musical numbers may not feel quite real to us, the feelings they communicate are real enough, and shape our sense of who characters are and what is important to their overall story.

The same is true of soundtracks generally. Occasionally a song or musical accompaniment has justification within the story, as when Alex turns on a cassette in his bedroom. They aren't, usually, a part of the story per se; instead they accompany it, expressing its mood. The same event, set to different songs, can take on wide variations in felt significance, from melancholic, to horrific, to exuberant. It is a very different experience to watch a horror film with the soundtrack muted. The sequence of events is the same, but the mood of the experience varies with the music. A telling example of the power of music is in a recut viral trailer of Kubrick's horror film *The Shining*, accompanied by Peter Gabriel's "Solsbury Hill," which turns it into an upbeat comedy about a writer in a rut who rediscovers the importance of fatherhood and family. Music adds an emotional tone to image sequences, and this can be done badly or well. Music can be cheap and sentimental, adding artificial gravity to a poorly developed narrative sequence. In the best instances, music accentuates or provides clues to the emotional tone that is already there in the images it accompanies. At the same time, as in the sequence under consideration now, music can work to undermine or offset our natural associations, creating an experience of emotional tension or confusion. When we associate a joyful song with a heinous act, the feeling of the song modifies our feelings of disgust at the act.

A related tension can appear when a voice doesn't fit its face. The high-pitched, whiny, nasal bray just can't, it seems, belong to the lovely black and white images of *Singin' in the Rain*'s Lina Lamont – who appears, to us, a different woman from the star she seems on screen. The scene that sets up the song "Singin' in the Rain" illustrates precisely both the disconnect between face and voice made possible through cinema, and the fact that the voice is itself a kind of face; it projects an image, what we expect to see. When they don't fit together the result is confusion and humor, as appeared in the disastrous reaction to the first screening of the non-musical "talkie" *The Dancing Cavalier*. When sound and voice do fit precisely, as in the opening image of *A*

Clockwork Orange, we don't even need to see lips moving to know that voice belongs to that face.

Let's return now to that face and that voice and to the opening scene that sets the tone for our experience of images to come. As the frame opens wide from Alex's stare and half-smile to encompass the bar, the voice begins to speak. "There was me, that is, Alex, and my three droogs, that is Pete, Georgie, and Dim, and we sat in the Korova Milk Bar, trying to make up our rassoodocks what to do with the evening." The voice speaks of what we witness at present as something in the past. It employs an unfamiliar vocabulary, but one not so distinct as to be indecipherable. What is clear from the image, at least from the intense, centered face and the listless and inattentive droogs beside him, is that no one else here but Alex is attempting to make up his rassoodock about anything. His next words make sense of the confusing writing on the walls that names the various types of drug-laced milk sold in the bar, and identifies the one that they were drinking ("Moloko Drencrom") and why (to sharpen them up for a night of violence). These words, which proceed from no one's mouth, are, in any case, not addressed to anyone else in the room. They are addressed to us; they introduce us to Alex and his world, inviting us to pay attention.

An address begs the question of who is being addressed, with perhaps greater urgency than, as already discussed, a look begs the question of just what it looks at. The voice that proceeds from no visible mouth and the face that looks out at no one in particular have here much the same function. There's no image within the frame that answers to that look, just as there's no one on screen to hear that address. We, therefore, must be the ones addressed by that voice and by that face. To make sense of the singer's look required that we pair that image with another image that appeared afterwards within the same frame, that of Alex raising his glass with a smile. To make sense of those faces is to imagine them facing one other. In the case of the opening image, though, there's no image to face it to, no ear to hear it. Whereas the singer's image pointed to another image currently out of view but within the same frame, the opening image points to what lies outside the frame entirely, without which it would not be an image at all but only colored light bouncing off of a white screen: the image's witness, the spectator. To make sense of this image is to feel oneself looked at by the image, to hear oneself addressed by that voice. We imagine the image facing us; we imagine the voice addressing us. At the same time, to confront this image is to encounter its frame, to see that it stands apart from us, and that we are not a part of it. We witness but cannot interact with this face; we hear but cannot respond to this voice. To witness, to bear witness, to describe, and assess are the only acts available to us in relation to the address of this image.

The image presents a face, and then shows us the person that face belongs to, engaged in actions throughout the night and what follows. The voice gives us context, motives, and meanings. His voice is expanded in song, by the music that accompanies his various activities and that express his attitudes towards what he does. At the same time, and throughout, we encounter other faces, of those who don't share Alex's feelings or sense of what matters, and to witness those faces is to encounter possibilities for assessing the same events differently. That Alex's voice, and his attitudes, aren't the only ones we're privy to suggests that the film as a whole is not reducible to a vehicle for his narration. The film as a whole presents a kind of face, an awareness of being looked at, distinct from that of Alex. It solicits our attention, and presents itself in a way that troubles our response to the viewpoint of Alex. Of course that's just to say that it was made so as to trouble us in that way, or that it manages to do it in any case.

The film does, prior to the opening sequence presenting Alex's face, announce in the title sequence that what follows is a film by Stanley Kubrick, which is to say that he takes responsibility for the final product, and might therefore be considered to provide the viewpoint for the film as a whole, distinct from that of Alex. In that case we might consider Kubrick as the one who poses questions in the film, by setting up and troubling a dominant viewpoint. Whether that's warranted or not, and it is far more likely to be warranted in Kubrick's case than in those of many other studio productions where the director takes credit, the effect of this credit on an audience is to encourage them to consider what follows in light of the director's other films, at least as much as compare it to films that might be otherwise similar, in subject matter or genre. The credit provides an additional point of reference, allowing audiences engaged in the film to make sense of what follows and sort out the questions it poses.

Kubrick does include at least one other direct reference to his prior body of work in the course of this film. Wandering through a music store, the day after his home invasion, Alex stops to ask a clerk about an order, while standing right next to the soundtrack album for *2001: A Space Odyssey*. This could be no more than a nod to his most famous prior film, and given that what we see is a soundtrack, it may signal the importance of music to both films. Still, given that both films present visions of the future, the inclusion entails at least that they are not meant to present the *same* future. In the world we imagine Alex to inhabit, *2001* was just a movie. If that movie has a message, it might be that technology had reached its peak when proto-humans learned to use tools as weapons, and that all subsequent developments have been merely refinements of the techniques whereby people wield power over people. The future depicted in *A Clockwork Orange* is less concerned with technological mastery and more with art and politics as means to social control.

The inclusion of this reference to this specific film within the film, as well as several other direct and indirect references to moviegoing in *A Clockwork Orange*, suggests that at least one issue explored within the film is the impact of images on those who witness them. The society depicted in *A Clockwork Orange* is apparently obsessed by images, and especially erotic imagery, from the naked statuary that adorns the Korova Milk Bar, to the graffiti-enhanced and Greek-inspired images of shirtless workmen in the lobby of Alex's building, to the phallic statue and erotic prints in the house of the woman Alex kills. In both the novel and the film, the slang word for "real fine" or "good" is "horrorshow" – which was, no doubt, derived by Burgess from the Russian "khorosho" but carries unmistakable overtones for Alex of the actual experience of watching violent and scary movies. He confirms this when, during his treatment, he's exposed to films depicting acts of violence, brutality, and rape. He describes the first film as "a very good professional piece of cine. Like it was done in Hollywood. The sounds were real horrorshow, you could slooshie the screams and moans very realistic." That the films resemble nothing so much as his actual daily activities outside of prison and his daydreams inside suggests that, for him at least, what is good is precisely what is encountered in such cinema. He declares, further, when blood starts to flow from the victim on screen, that "It was beautiful. It's funny how the colors of the real world only seem real when you viddy them on screen."

What we see on screen is both like the real world and shapes how we see things outside of the screen. It offers more than just a copy of reality, since it also offers ideals, in relation to which we measure realities and consider them deficient. Films have the power to transform our sense of how things are and what matters. They are a part of reality, but stand apart. Movies make sense to us, we understand them, in much the same way as we understand anything. Yet in our reflections upon their ways of making sense to us, we can become aware of the active role we play in making sense of anything. We have considered a number of the significant forms employed in cinema, some of which draw upon our ordinary capacities to make sense of anything, such as our recognition of faces and what they reveal and conceal. Others, such as the use of the frame or the edit or styles of movement, employ conventions distinctive to the medium of film. Making sense of cinema is not merely an exercise in thinking, it is above all something felt, and nowhere is the impact of mood on meaning clearer than in considerations of the use of music in film. At the same time, films can push audiences to ask questions, to reflect upon and relate what they see directly to what they know from outside of the film, as well as to reflect upon the experience itself of watching film.

The self-reflexive elements in this film make it, as most challenging films are, something of an intellectual puzzle: with no end of questions it enables exploring, including questions about itself and about the very medium of film, and about its impact on its audience. We'll continue to explore some such questions in what follows. If anything is distinctive to the body of work attributed to Stanley Kubrick it is the combination of intensely visceral subject matter, artistically rendered so as to raise concerns of the highest abstraction. His works are both conceptually rigorous and artistically provocative. In Kubrick's films, art and ideas are intertwined, and this poses an important challenge to an ancient tradition that pits an art that deals images against philosophy and ideas. To see the weight of this challenge, and the extent to which it can be met, we'll turn now to a consideration of the philosopher who made its case most strongly. Plato has Socrates argue in the *Republic* that certain kinds of artists – among whom would likely fall filmmakers, if they had existed in his day – should be banned from the ideal city, for reasons we might compare to those that had *A Clockwork Orange* banned from Britain. We'll return to *A Clockwork Orange* later to examine one of the most famous images from that film, the image of Alex "in treatment," which bears an uncanny resemblance to one of Plato's own most famous images in the *Republic*, the allegory of the cave. First we'll consider that image and its significance in some detail.

2 Plato's cave and cinema

Philosophy has almost always had a troubled relationship with art, and especially with those artworks aimed to entertain the masses. Plato's *Republic*, written in the age of ancient Greece, describes an (even then) ancient quarrel between philosophy and poetry, where "poetry" was understood to encompass storytelling, theater, and other popular arts. At the same time – and this may account for the conflict's endurance – there are remarkable affinities between philosophy and art. Even in its most popular genres art engages with our deepest values and highest aspirations. The arts explore ideals in sensuous and concrete form. Ancient theater and poetry, for example, depict characters whose struggles resonate with their audience, because what they strive for is what we all strive for to some degree or other: love, a better life, honor, beauty, dignity, revenge, freedom, justice, an enduring legacy, truth. Philosophy, in its own way, approaches just these issues: what is love, what is the best kind of life, what is honor, what is justice, what is freedom, what is beauty, what is truth and how do we attain it? It is ironic, perhaps, but no accident that Plato himself, whose writings posed what is perhaps the most serious and still relevant challenge to poetry and popular art, nevertheless wrote down his own philosophy in the form of dramatic dialogues, depicting characters whose struggles were for understanding, who grappled with ideas. In spite of their heady themes, when read with care his dialogues can be quite entertaining, and exhibit the marks of a master of dramatic craft. There is a careful attention to setting. There is subtlety in the subtexts. There is comedy in the human foibles of his characters who struggle not to seem ridiculous, there is pathos in the realization that what matters most to them may not be worth having, there is tragedy in the discovery that the human condition may render ideals unattainable.

In the past few decades the popular art of film has captured the imagination of philosophers precisely for its capacity to dramatize ideas that might otherwise appear abstract, disconnected from the concerns of everyday life. Films entertain not only by leading us to care about characters and their conflicts, or to be fascinated and swept away by spectacle, but also by calling upon us to explore and entertain thoughts regarding questions we cannot help but take seriously, because they are the questions around which we shape the significance of our lives. One might even speculate that were Plato alive today, he'd be a filmmaker, enacting his philosophy through the medium of film. It is hard to say what such films might look like, but they'd likely exploit the power of cinema to capture the living character of conversation, with all of its subtleties and subtexts and contextual clues intact. They'd likely hold up on first viewing, and also stand the test of time, revealing layers of depth and intricacies of insight. Their richest teachings would require an active and engaged audience, ready to think alongside and beyond what was explicitly stated, to complete thoughts only half-spoken, to pursue lines of inquiry that are hinted at but left unexamined by the characters on screen.

We might suppose a Platonic cinema would be unlikely to focus on the sheer spectacle of the screen. Still, one only needs to look to the *Apology*, where Socrates defends his life before a crowd of assembled Athenians, or the *Phaedo*, a work set in an Athenian prison as Socrates prepares for his execution, weeping friends by his side, in order to see that Plato was no stranger to the importance of situating conversation in an appropriately vivid dramatic setting. In spite of concerns raised in the *Republic* and elsewhere about the danger of images, and their power to influence attitudes and ideas without reason, Plato was in fact quite skilled at creating images with his words, images that continue both to fascinate and instruct. One can only speculate what kinds of images he'd create for the screen, but we can compare the immersive experience of cinema directly with one of the most powerful images in Plato's works, the allegory of the cave.

Shadows on the wall

In his *Republic* Plato depicts his teacher Socrates engaged in conversation with various friends and acquaintances regarding ethics, justice, and politics. To clarify the importance and impact of a philosophical education, he asks his interlocutors to imagine a cave, full of prisoners chained from birth and compelled to look at a shadowy spectacle unfolding upon the cavern wall before them. Behind these prisoners lies a concealed pathway, and along the path a strange procession of men carrying statues. The statues, made of stone or wood, and the like, are formed in the likenesses of men and other animals, and the men who carry them walk along the path, sometimes silent, sometimes speaking. Farther along in the cave there is a large bonfire, whose light casts shadows of these moving statues upon the wall of the cave which the prisoners face. So for their entire lives, all that these prisoners encounter are the flickering shadows, and the echoes from the speakers on the road seem to come to them from the shadows themselves. If the prisoners were to speak, their words would ring hollow; if they were to argue, it would be over phantoms.

Before going on, take a look at the allegory in Plato's own words, which appears at the beginning of Book VII of the *Republic*. Note that in the following passage Socrates is the speaker (the "I" of the discourse), and, while several others are present and listening, it is Plato's brother Glaucon who provides the responses (the "he" of the discourse).

> "Next then," I said, "make an image of our nature in its education and want of education, likening it to a condition of the following kind. See human beings as though they were in an underground cave-like dwelling with its entrance, a long one, open to the light across the whole width of the cave. They are in it from childhood with their legs and necks in bonds so that they are fixed, seeing only in front of them, unable because of the bond to turn their heads all the way around. Their light is from a fire burning far above and behind them. Between the fire and the prisoners there is a road above, along which see a wall, built like the partitions puppet-handlers set in front of the human beings and over which they show the puppets."
>
> "I see," he said.
>
> "Then also see along this wall human beings carrying all sorts of artifacts, which project above the wall, and statues of men and other animals wrought from stone, wood, and every kind of material; as is to be expected, some of the carriers utter sounds while others are silent."
>
> "It's a strange image," he said, "and strange prisoners you're telling of."
>
> "They're like us," I said.
>
> (514a–515a)

Socrates explains that the men in the cave see nothing of themselves or each other, only shadows cast by statues on the wall in front of them. Their heads are bound motionless, but they can hear each other's voices. The only other sounds they hear are echoes from the puppeteers who parade behind them, which they consider to be voices and sounds from the shadows before them, the only reality they know. As he concludes:

> "Then most certainly," I said, "such men would hold that the truth is nothing other than the shadows of artificial things."
>
> (515c)

It is a strange image. An image of us, claims Socrates, an allegory of the human condition in the absence of a genuine philosophical education. What we take to be most real, what we encounter all around us, is like shadows on a wall, and our so-called common sense and understanding of the world is nothing more than prejudice, untrustworthy opinions rooted in false assumptions. Instead of honest inquiry into the way things really are, we are more concerned with debate, aimed at silencing critics. This ancient image may appear, however, to resemble not so much the human condition generally but that of watching with an audience films on a large screen in a darkened theater. We wait in line and purchase tickets, buy popcorn and candy, then enter into a large chamber where we sit on cushioned seats, captive and captivated for a couple of hours as a spectacle projects upon the lightened screen before us. Or, we turn down the lights and sit on a couch with family and friends and watch movies or TV on a large, flat-screen, high-definition television. The shadowy processions are projected, in this case, not from men carrying statues, but from the activities of people and things whose movements have become framed and fixed like sculptures in time by the artistry and mechanisms of photography and video.

It is an obvious comparison, and modern readers of the *Republic* often consider Plato to have anticipated cinema in his description of the rightly famous allegory of the cave. There are, yet, important differences. Moviegoers can leave their seats, exit the theater, into the light. They arrive at the theater with memories drawn from outside, and compare what they see there with what they've seen and encountered elsewhere. In Plato's cave, by contrast, the prisoners have no access to any other kind of experience than the shadows they witness and echoes that appear to them to emanate from the cavern wall, until, that is, they are released from the shackles and educated. Even that's not strictly correct. The prisoners must also feel their own bodies, and even in chains they presumably can open and shut their own eyes. Socrates even says that they speak to one another, and argue over what they see. So they are aware, at least, of something other than echoes and shadows. They are aware of their own bodies, and they are aware of others beside them, who share their language and see the same things they do. Still, unlike modern moviegoers, they are unaware of anywhere else, or anything else than what they witness together by the flickering light of the flames in the darkened cavern they've inhabited all their lives.

Plato's allegory is intended to illuminate the nature of human experience generally, while our fascination with films and television (and with other moving images online), however widespread and frequent, occupies only a portion of our time and attention. The uncanny resemblances between the particular experience of watching film and the image Plato employs to highlight features of ordinary experience, however, make them worth comparing, to see whether the peculiar nature of film watching can be clarified thereby, and whether film might itself serve to clarify something of the nature of experience in general. Also, given that the allegory is intended to illuminate the nature of a philosophical education, a comparison with film may also serve to suggest just what it might mean for film to be philosophical.

For a fuller picture of the condition of the prisoners, and a clearer understanding of how it relates to ordinary experience, and in order to prepare for a further comparison with the experience of watching movies, we should explore Plato's allegory further. Socrates makes clear that the prisoners, and by extension us, acquire opinions about the world not just through sensation. We don't just look on and learn. We talk about what we see and hear and sense. We argue about what we've seen. We try to convince others what we'll see in the future. We form opinions not only based on sense, but on "common sense," which is another phrase for communal prejudice. Socrates imagines what might happen if someone were dragged out of the cave unwillingly, and learned what things are really like, and suggests that if that person were to return he'd see clearly how ill-founded are the usual procedures whereby the cave's prisoners come to know the world. Not only do they argue over what they've seen, what they're seeing, and what they'll see, but they also compete, giving honors and prizes for those whose accounts are most convincing.

The following passage continues from where we left off. Here Socrates imagines a prisoner being released and then returning to the cave with a whole new perspective.

> "Now consider," I said, "what their release and healing from bonds and folly would be like if something of this sort were by nature to happen to them. Take a man who is released and suddenly compelled to stand up, to turn his neck around, to walk and look up toward the light; and who, moreover, in doing all this is in pain and, because he is dazzled, is unable to make out those things whose

shadows he saw before. What do you suppose he'd say if someone
were to tell him that before he saw silly nothings, while now,
because he is somewhat nearer to what is and more turned toward
beings, he sees more correctly; and, in particular, showing him each
of the things that pass by, were to command the man to answer his
questions about what they are? Don't you suppose he'd be at a loss
and believe that what was seen before is truer than what is now
shown?"

"Yes," he said, "by far."

"And, if he compelled him to look at the light itself, would his
eyes hurt and would he flee, turning away to those things that he
is able to make out and hold them to be really clearer than what is
being shown?"

"So he would," he said.

(515c–e)

Socrates suggests that the prisoner would resist his release, and need to
be dragged up and out of the cave against his will. At first unable to see
anything at all by the light of the sun, he'd have to get used to seeing
shadows once again, and then images in water, and eventually things
themselves. Only after all of this would he be able to catch a glimpse of
the sun itself, and discover that everything visible depends upon it. He
would recognize the folly of his former companions in the cave, and be
reluctant to return.

"And if in that time there were among them any honors, praises,
and prizes for the man who is sharpest at making out the things that
go by, and most remembers which of them are accustomed to pass
before, which after, and which at the same time as the others, and
who is thereby most able to divine what is going to come, in your
opinion would he be desirous of them and envy those who are
honored and hold power among these men? Or, rather, would he be
affected as Homer says and want very much 'to be on the soil, a serf
to another man, to a portionless man,' and to undergo anything
whatsoever rather than to opine those things and live that way?"

"Yes," he said, "I suppose he would prefer to undergo everything
rather than live that way."

(516c–d)

For now let us look past the significance of the released prisoner, who is
dragged out of the cave and eventually sees the truth by the light of the
sun; skip to the end of the allegory, where the former prisoner returns to

the cave and sees with new eyes the condition he'd shared with the others before his release. Comparing what he sees then with what we've seen already can give us a fuller picture of the initial condition inside the cave, which Socrates likens to the ordinary experience of all of us prior to an encounter with philosophy.

Note the games that the prisoners play. They honor and give prizes to those who can best remember, perceive, and predict the play of shadows. Given that in the case of a dispute there is no way to decide what really did take place or what will, the prize seems likely to go to the one who has the loudest voice, or is most capable of persuading others of the spin he puts on things. Socrates proposes that such games – which might be thought to resemble talk shows in which competing commentators give their opinionated takes on past and current events – would hold little interest for the prisoner who'd seen what was really going on. Still, for us, it is interesting to note that these games of memory, identification, and prediction mirror precisely what is involved in ordinary perception. Plato's allegory suggests, moreover, a significant dimension of ordinary perception that is often overlooked: that we perceive the world along with others, that what we perceive is the same world as they do, even if our perspectives differ, and that the process of deciphering just what it is we perceive is a social process, carried on with those others with whom we communicate.

To perceive anything at all, it is not enough just to open your eyes, listen, feel around, taste, and smell. The world we perceive is a world of change, always in flux. To perceive something specific involves picking it out from amongst the flux. One must, as Socrates notes, learn to "make out the things that go by," identifying each thing in distinction from the others, attributing to each thing its salient sensible properties: a red car flashing by, a signal turned green, a sudden dark thing darting out onto the road in front of me, requiring me to swerve to avoid hitting whatever it was with my car. The infant develops as she comes to identify objects of interest to her, out from the frantic flow of sensations; she shows her perceptual grasp of significant objects by reaching for and grasping selectively. It is not enough, though, just to identify objects by their sensible properties, because the objects we perceive come and go, and undergo change.

Perception involves recognition. We must recall what we have seen before, and learn to notice when what we now see is the same as what came before. Perception, then, involves a conception of "the same" and "the different," of a "before" and "now" and "after," of a "thing" that is the same as it undergoes change, and thus a conception of a difference between the "what" a thing is and the "how" of its appearing, which amounts to a rudimentary conception of the difference between a thing and its sensible properties. Perception involves a capacity to identify and name objects, to distinguish between the object and its momentary appearance, so as to recognize as the same an object that has undergone change. When we have recognized things from out of the flux of changing sensations, when we have become familiar with them and their properties, we also anticipate what they will do next, we begin to make predictions regarding the future, so that perception also entails our coming to expect that things will behave as the kinds of things we think they are. The general form of this expectation amounts to a primitive conception of causality that needn't be deterministic but certainly holds that things don't happen arbitrarily. To see what we take to be a dog is to expect it will behave as a dog. In general, to identify anything as an X is to expect it will behave in the way that we think that Xs do.

All of this should be more or less familiar as an account of what goes on in ordinary perception – whether in the world at large or in a darkened theater watching movies. It does make clear that there is more going on in perception than merely looking on. To perceive is to be operating with ideas – of identity and difference, of before and after, of the difference between a thing and its manifest properties, and more specific ideas that allow us to recognize things for what they are – ideas that are not themselves sensed, but are conditions for sensing, and thus must exist for us independently of this or that sensation. We should note, in particular, that while we can be mistaken in our particular identifications – as when we think that this or that appearance is the same as another – the mistake itself relies upon a stable and unmistakable conception of identity.

What is especially provocative, though, and, perhaps for that reason, largely overlooked or ignored by modern readers of the *Republic*, is the suggestion in Plato's allegory that this entire perceptual process of identification, recognition, familiarization, and prediction takes place in a competitive social context. Plato simply does not hold that we make sense of the world on our own. From the very beginning our perception of the world is mediated by language and by social discourse. From early on we interact with others as we learn to make sense of the world; and these early interactions are not neutral, as we start out in relations of complete dependence upon those who tell us stories, teach us to speak, and otherwise assist us in identifying what is significant in the world around us.

The allegory of the cave suggests a very different picture of perception than the one we have inherited from modern philosophy beginning with Descartes, according to which each of us begins as an isolated subject whose perspective on the world is closed off from that of others. The cave is not, as some have suggested, primarily a metaphor for the individual mind. According to the allegory, perception is not private but public. The shadows are not in our heads, but out there around us, and we are not alone in the cave, but with others. The shadows on the wall are the same for each of the prisoners; even if one of them views things from a slightly different angle, they are in the same room, with the same light source, seeing the same shadows on the same wall. Likewise in everyday life we encounter the same world, with roughly the same perceptual capacities, and we learn to make sense of it together by talking about what we have encountered, what we are encountering now, and what we expect to find next.

Socrates knows it is unlikely the prisoners would escape (and approach philosophy) on their own. The chains of familiarity and social pressure that keep them (and us) from thinking otherwise than in accordance with common sense – which insists there's nothing more to reality than what we see on the surface and that consensus is the mark of true belief – are far too strong. We need to be turned around – but not in the literal sense, as occurs in the allegory, when a prisoner is released and dragged out of the cave forcibly. The escape from the cave is a metaphor for learning to adopt a wholly new perspective on what appears to us – it does not suggest there's some other place one might go in order to know the truth. The cave is the human condition: shadows (or appearances) are all we're ever going to perceive. We need to have our souls turned around – which means we need to be pushed to look at the same things but differently. We need to be shown, specifically, that appearance is not identical with reality, and that persuasion and consensus do not entail truth. We need to see that our assessments of appearances, our decisions regarding how things have turned out and how things ought to turn out, are rooted in ideals that often amount to no more than ill-founded judgments, that may or may not serve our interests, and whose ultimate worth is often untested. To escape from the cave is to learn to adopt an interrogative attitude toward appearances. Others might say, "Look at that face," and the philosopher will ask "Just what is a face?" and not merely with the intent of being difficult but because, as we have seen, to be a face is to be something quite remarkable and strange when you consider it, altogether different from a mere object. Even mere objects can harbor unanticipated depths for those who consider them with care. Others pass the judgment: "this is beautiful" or "this is just." The philosopher asks: "what is justice?" and "what is beauty?" such that those assertions can make sense.

Socrates draws the following surprising lesson from the allegory of the cave. "Education is not what the professions of certain men assert it to be. They presumably assert that they put into the soul knowledge that isn't in it, as though they were putting sight into blind eyes" (*Republic*, 518b). A genuine education, according to Socrates, is not a matter of instilling new knowledge into empty minds. As Socrates never tires of insisting in nearly every Platonic dialogue in which he appears: the work of philosophy does not so much consist of imparting new knowledge, new concepts, and new ways of thinking. It is, rather, a matter of drawing out and making clear what is already known and taken for granted. Philosophy heeds the challenge posed by T.S. Elliot in his *Four Quartets*: "We shall not cease from exploration | And the end of all our exploring | Will be to arrive where we started | And know the place for the first time."

The resources for initiating the philosophical turn are already contained within us, within ordinary experience. We are, in the terms of the allegory, dragged out of the cave by means of the very same chains that keep us there. What holds us in the cave, enthralled to appearances, is common sense and popular opinion. To be turned around and dragged out of the cave is to be forced to examine the assumptions we take for granted and shown they can't withstand the light of day. It is also to be shown that even our diverging opinions regarding appearances rest on shared underlying structures of understanding that can be elucidated. Socrates suggests that there is

> an art of this turning around, concerned with the way in which this power can be most easily and efficiently turned around, not an art of producing sight in it. Rather, this art takes as given that sight is there, but not rightly turned, nor looking at what it ought to look at, and accomplishes this object.
>
> (*Republic*, 518d)

The examination of our opinions and principles takes place, for Socrates, in the medium of language, and his art, the Socratic method, is to ask questions about how things seem to his listeners and then to ask questions about the answers they provide, encouraging them to make clarifying distinctions, in order to show them in the end that their assumptions are inconsistent or that they cannot account for all the appearances, and to lead them to look into themselves and to listen to others in the quest for better answers. A Socratic education goes from opinions regarding what is evident, to a critical investigation of the presumed standards upon which the opinions are based, toward insight into the principles that underlie and render any critical investigation possible.

Socrates makes the stages on the way explicit in his discussion of the divided line, which describes various ways of knowing and their objects, beginning with the entertaining of images and ending in a glimpse of "the Good." While philosophy begins with the way things seem, its aim is to grasp how they really are and ought to be, and how this impacts us and who we are and should aspire to be. To pursue this is to be on the track of what he calls "the Good." We say of many things they are good, and nearly everything is good for something. What good things share, what it is that makes them good, he says, is an idea, a "good itself," not exclusive to any of them or reducible to their sum. At first, this doesn't seem to follow. The "good" in each could be different, as fast cars are good for getting somewhere, and classical music good to listen to, but getting somewhere fast and listening to a symphony are very different, even if Alex enjoys doing both. Not everything good is enjoyable either, and what is good for some isn't good for others. What he means, then, by "the Good" can't be just a generic quality of everything good, since there may not be anything all so-called goods have in common.

Admitting it is not clear how there can be just one idea of the Good that accounts for the multiplicity of goods, he sets up an analogy between the Good and the sun. Just as the sun makes it possible to see things, the Good lets them be understood. What's more, as the sun gives light to the diversity of living things so they can grow and flourish together on the very same Earth, the Good gives life to ideas, the way they really are and ought to be, as they are thinkable together. The comparison rests, first of all, upon a distinction between things as they appear, and as they can be thought. For simplicity's sake, he focuses on the visual appearance of things, contrasting this with their intelligibility. The distinction, while profound in its implications, is fairly straightforward – in fact it is like the difference we've seen between the many good things and the Good itself. There are many cars and lots of classical music, but what makes them cars and music, what it is to be a car or music, must itself be known in order to recognize any of them for what it is, and to appraise its quality as what it is. To know this is to know its "form" or "idea." It is more than a definition, because it's not just a matter of how we use words but of getting clear what we're talking about; and it is not just a matter of seeing what things are but of thinking what they ought to be. We don't just identify cars and music; we appraise them, and consider them better and worse based on whether they live up to what we consider it possible for them to be.

Now we can't say in advance what is possible for a symphony or car, and none of them count as the best it could be. The idea of a car, then, is not so much a definition but, as suggested, takes the form of a question, a provocation to thought: "just what is a car? (What could it be? What should it be?)" It is not a clueless question, however, as to ask it intelligently requires that at minimum we recognize cars. It is not just an idea either, in the narrow sense of just a thought in someone's head, since there really are cars and there really is something it is to be a car, and not just anything fits. To understand anything, though, to see it for what it is, whether composition or car or institution or animal, is to recognize it both as what it is and not fully what it could be. It is to grasp it as a kind of thing that's not exhausted by or fully realized in any of its instances. Additionally, and this is key, the good of each will in some way relate to the good of another. A completely new car, that lets us see what is possible in cars and sets a new standard for their excellence, may also require a new kind of fuel or a new kind of road, as it wouldn't be any good to have a car that couldn't go anywhere. We could always ask, further, how the new roads and the new cars impact the forms of commerce and community they connect, and whether that impact is for the better. To consider, of anything, what it is and ought to be, requires that we also have some notion of how the many goods hang together, a grip of the whole, what that is and ought to be. We can in fact find an example of this kind of inquiry in the *Republic*, where the many good things that participate in community have to be considered together, for their impact on each other. The final definition of justice in the dialogue, not coincidentally, turns out to involve each of the many members of the community doing their own thing well, in such a way as to contribute to the good of all and each.

It is, roughly, this unity of the many goods, the positing of which makes it possible for us to think them all together, that Socrates refers to when he speaks of the Good. To clarify the notion of "the Good," he compares it to something familiar: the sun that illuminates and warms and gives life to the many things we can see. The sun's light is what renders things visible; without it, living things, at least, couldn't exist. The Good's presence, both in our thoughts and in things, renders them not only intelligible but also possible. Unless our thinking hangs together, nothing really ends up making sense. Except as realities hang together, mutually serving one another's needs, making each other possible and the whole together intact, nothing really could end up at all. The attempt to think things through together, sorting out their mutual implications and eliminating those conceptions that cannot coexist, depends on our holding that things do and must hang together as a whole. Ideas of the many can be thought through only under the guidance of the idea of ideas, which is not just one of the many ideas but stands above them and in some sense rules them all, the idea of the Good.

To spell it out further, Socrates asks his interlocutors to imagine a line, divided in two, representing the difference between what can be seen, on the one hand, and what is understood, on the other. The first is ruled over by the sun; the latter by the Good. The first part of the line he subdivides further, into two classes of the visible. There are, first, images or appearances, as, for example, the shadows of four droogs that appear under a bridge before they are seen directly, or even the image of them coming into the light, or the way they look from the side or behind or right up face-to-face. Then there are the things themselves that are depicted or appear, such as the droogs themselves if they happened to exist, who could take on a range of appearances depending on how they stand or how we stand in relation to them, and on whether they're wearing eyelashes and makeup, masks, or hats.

Socrates, later, links the first level of images with the shadows in the cave, and the things they are images of with the statues. It should, therefore, be clear that according to Plato what we deal with for the most part in our everyday encounters are not things themselves, but how they appear to us, which is the result both of sensation and imagination. What we imagine, how we link up current appearances with the past and what we anticipate for future interactions with them, is a product both of our idiosyncratic backgrounds, private fantasies, and hopes and dreams, as well as our collective sense of how things are and what is important. We see things from a narrow point of view, and we connect what we see with what we've seen before and heard of elsewhere. Even when we deal with things more directly, when in our interactions with them they challenge our sense of what they are and ought to be, we still have to do only with those aspects they reveal to us partially, what we are prepared to notice and address. In our dealings with images or appearances, we are, at best, operating only on the level of opinion, and at worst with private fantasies, or with the shared sense of how things are that is reinforced by propaganda and power, and that we sometimes call ideology.

He divides the second part of the line into ideas and principles, the highest of which is the Good itself. For the first he suggests we begin with things, and consider what they really are and ought to be by way of hypotheses. Math is his example: it is not about this or that triangle or line or quantity of items, but usually starts there, with a figure on a chalkboard, and the effort to define it. One might hold up a clock or an orange or draw a circle on the board, but what is then considered is what is true of any circle or any sphere or any shape whatsoever. To get there, they form definitions and postulates as hypotheses and consider what follows from them, and in their deductions aim above all at clarity and consistency. The orange itself is complicated, and can be considered from a number of perspectives; the mathematician considers it only insofar as it conforms to the definition and exhibits the properties of a specific and well-defined shape. While this is obviously the arena of math and geometry, this general approach to thinking is the starting point for any inquiry that aims to go beyond confused opinions based on appearances and rooted in collective prejudice. We start with things and pose questions about them, positing definitions as provisional answers and making distinctions and seeing what follows and whether it fits. When we drop a provisional postulate or revise a definition that shows up insufficient, we learn more about the thing, making our idea of what it is and can and ought to be more vivid. It is only when we change the conversation, from how things seem to us to consider how we do and ought to define them, that we move beyond the pleasant or heated exchange of opinions, in which nothing real can come to light.

What guides such inquiry are principles – such as the idea that what is inconsistent can't be true, what is false should be rejected, what is shameful or ugly should be abjured, and what is unjust should be corrected – tacitly presumed at first and later coming into clarity themselves as the true starting points of our thinking. The inquiry into principles themselves – of which we see examples in Plato's dialogues, which ask about knowledge, justice, beauty, and truth – forms the highest part of the divided line. Even where we disagree about what is true and what is right, we can't but agree that what is false should not be believed and what is wrong should not be done. In the *Republic* a range of hypotheses about the institutions and laws of the ideal city are considered and rejected because they turn out to be unjust or inconsistent. Even Thrasymachus, who in the first book urged that what ordinary people think just really serves only the interests of the powerful, considered it truly just for the most powerful to rule by any means necessary, and so he never seriously urged injustice. We let go of hypotheses, because they are inconsistent either with each other or with our larger principles, or because however valid they might seem on their own, holding them alongside one another turns out to be impossible. Philosophy aims to move up the ladder, from appearances to things; from things to hypotheses aimed at getting clear about the nature of things, what they are, and what they ought to be; from hypotheses to principles, toward clarity regarding the ultimate values that underlie our various claims and assessments regarding people, institutions, and things.

Projecting the light

It is worth considering whether there might be another art – not exclusively verbal – that accomplishes a similar shift in the way appearances are understood. Could there be an art that not only employs language in an effort to raise questions regarding assumptions and to motivate a new perspective on given appearances, but that also creates and delivers new appearances, linking them together in ways that lead us to see things differently? It might seem obvious that film has the capacity to be such an art. Recall, though, that watching movies resembles the situation of the prisoners in the cave, which Socrates describes in order to illustrate the condition of life in the absence of philosophy. The condition of the prisoners, seated in a darkened chamber, watching moving shadows and flickering lights, and hearing echoes (recordings) of fading voices, resembles closely the experience of watching films in a theater, where the audience is not so much captive but captivated by the story and spectacle unfolding before it. Still, there is an important difference, as we've already noted, between the condition of Plato's prisoners and the condition of the audience at a film. Filmgoers know that what they're watching isn't real. They can compare what they see on screen with how they think things really are, and ask questions about the differences. If we imagine that the procession of statues in Plato's cave is not random but deliberate, directed by an artist whose aim is to alert the prisoners to their captive condition, employing techniques to signal his artifice, then we might consider this shadow play to be analogous to a philosophical cinema. In this case, we might say, film approaches the condition of philosophy, insofar as it leads audiences to reflect upon appearances, to reflect upon conditions we inhabit in the cave.

The cinema does not always lead audiences to question appearances. More often and more likely it serves to inculcate the very assumptions that philosophy would call into question. It is widely held (does that mean it's true?) that film and television both create and reinforce some of our most strongly held stereotypes. This would suggest that film (along with other arts) might function like the chains in Plato's cave. Film would serve as a counterforce to philosophy, discouraging reflection, encouraging acceptance of appearances, and reinforcing stereotypes. It is just this kind of concern that, as we'll see, Socrates fleshes out in his various criticisms of poetic art in the *Republic*. Can film be both a counterforce to thought, one that strengthens chains that bind us to appearances and prejudice, and a liberating agent that encourages the kind of reflective transformation that is philosophy? First, consider the comparison between Plato's allegory of the cave and cinema. We'll examine Plato's critique of the storytelling arts later, and consider also the extent to which film or at least some films such as *A Clockwork Orange* can address and overcome the concerns he raises.

The core components of Socrates' account of the initial stage of the cave can be compared directly to elements of the cinematic experience. There are, first, the prisoners, who appear not to know they are bound. Next, what takes place behind them, a strange procession carrying statues whose shadows (and echoes) are projected onto (and bounced off of) the wall by the light of a crackling bonfire. Finally, the shadow play itself and the echoes from the activity behind them, all witnessed by the prisoners.

The play of shadows and echoes compares to the film itself as it appears when projected onto or presented by way of a screen. The actual film is not the celluloid strip or the DVD or digital file, but is what results from their projection or screening, an audio-visual presentation that unfolds as a sequence in time, that shows entities moving about and making sounds. At the very least – and setting aside for the moment experimental films like those of Stan Brakhage, who often painted and pasted elements directly on film strips to create his arresting imagery – what is seen on screen are objects or entities that persist in space and time and undergo change and movement. For the most part, audiences understand these movements as actions, motivated movements that gradually make sense as developments within an ongoing story. Usually, and in the most general terms, the story presents someone who wants something or other, and something gets in the way, requiring the agent to rise to the occasion or fail or otherwise transform the initial situation.

The prisoners compare to the audience, seated in the darkened theater on cushioned seats, not captive but captivated by the spectacle unfolding before them. Stories grip their audiences, and work as stories, only to the extent the audience comes to care what happens to the characters. They can, of course, unlike the prisoners, exit the theater. They also come to the experience with an awareness of the difference between what they see on screen and the objects and intrigues they encounter outside. Important as these differences may seem, however, they can be overstressed. Audiences enter the cinema by choice, but once a movie starts there is a presumption they will stick around to the end; to get up and leave amounts to a critical response to the film as a whole, made public by the very act of leaving the theater, and the finality of this pronouncement is one most aren't prepared to deliver until they've seen the film through to the finish. Most want to know how things end up, and can't say for sure whether the film delivered on its promise until then. If we enter with friends, there's at least potentially a tacit betrayal or disruption of their experience; they will wonder why we left and whether our assessment of the film amounts to a critical evaluation of their taste. It is somewhat different in the privacy of one's living room, where changing the channel carries less critical weight. One can always turn it back or catch it later in another mood.

Whether we watch films in the cinema, or alone in our homes, can make a significant difference. Even in a darkened theater, we are aware of the presence of others, whose laughter and gasps do help shape our response to the film. Like Plato's prisoners, whose perception is social, our sense of what matters on screen, how to take it and what it means, is inevitably informed by the reactions of others. What might be frightening alone can become a farce if everyone's giggling. It's not only, though, what we hear and see around us that affects us. Recalling the judgments of others, both friends and movie critics, and anticipating the reactions of a loved one, can modify our appreciation to a significant degree. What we think about it, in the moment, is inseparable from our expectations of subsequent sharing.

Moreover, while audience members watch this or that movie by choice, and can at least in principle get up and leave or change the channel, they can't choose, we might say, whether or not to belong to a culture that is deeply informed by the clichés and conventions of television and cinema. Most of us come of age as members of a captive audience, and later come to embrace our chains. In that sense we belong to cinema, as much as it belongs to us. The cinematic experience belongs to and is to a large degree continuous with the rest of our everyday lives. It has distinctive features, but is no more disconnected from everyday living than, say, talking on the phone or driving a car, or talking on the phone while driving a car. For those who drive cars and own phones and watch movies, these are permanent possibilities that both fit into and form part of everyday life, and also transform it from what it would be without them.

The procession of statues, projected onto the cavern wall by a flickering light, compares to the entire apparatus of cinema, the industry responsible for the production and distribution of films, and the technologies responsible for projecting them onto a screen. We might consider the apparatus of cinema as providing material conditions for the film experience. It is significant, though, that what the prisoners witness, what they consider to be reality, is in fact the result of deliberate activities on the part of those who created the statues and march along behind them. One important difference between the audiences of cinema and the prisoners in the cave is that cinematic audiences are, at least to some degree, aware of the artificial character of what they witness. They know that what they see on screen was made, and could have been otherwise. With respect to the rest of their experience, however, they (and we) are arguably in the same condition as the prisoners in the cave, as they take their common-sense interpretations of what they encounter to be the way things simply are. Perhaps what we need to learn, and what a comparison between the allegory of the cave and the experience of cinema makes clear, is to see our everyday lives as analogous with cinema. Rather than considering the cinema unreal by comparison with everyday life, the comparison of everyday life with cinema should remind us that what we encounter around us is merely appearance, that our assumptions about what we take to be most real are contingent and revisable.

More important than the material apparatus, the technology and artifice of cinema, is what we might call its intelligible dimension. Light, what gives shape to the shadows and makes them visible in the first place, can be compared to the meaningful character of cinema, the forms and conventions that enable what is on screen to be interpreted and understood. Light is not itself the object of vision – it is what enables objects to be viewed, and exists independently of this or that viewed object or viewer. It is what links the audience, apparatus, and image, and without it there can be no vision. Projected onto the wall and perceived by the audience, it gives rise to the image, which can only be in being perceived. The technology and artifice of cinema is always, to the extent that the filmmakers are competent, in the service of the significance of the moving image, which is thus of paramount importance in considerations of its experience.

To be discerned at all, the shadows need to have a determinate shape, and their movements need to be roughly continuous. If there were no discernible rhythm or flow to the movements of the shadows, the prisoners would be at a loss to say anything at all about them. There would be, literally, nothing to talk about. At the same time, their words would themselves be empty, without meaning for them, unless they could remember what they'd seen, unless they could differentiate between distinct shapes, and identify recurring shapes. Likewise for cinematic images, if there were no discernible links between one projected frame and the next, if there were no recurring patterns, if every time a spectator entered the cinema she had no idea what to expect and walked out having no idea what she'd seen, there wouldn't be anything to the cinematic experience.

Note that the intelligibility of cinema is not something that belongs to this or that film, or even to film as a whole. It isn't something, either, that resides in the technological apparatus, or merely in the minds of the spectators. Just as light is not itself directly seen but is what brings seer and seen together in the first place, the intelligibility of cinema resides in the relation between the audience and the film, a relationship that is shaped by the audience's physiology, their past, their culture, their encounters with film, and their everyday experience. As a result of all of this we can say what we're seeing, and what we're seeing makes sense. It makes sense to us because there's continuity to what we see, because what we see has a discernible shape and character, and because we can link up what we see now to what we've seen before. What we encounter, for the most part, is not the "blooming buzzing confusion," which the psychologist and philosopher William James described as the experience of infants. We recognize what we hear and see; we identify objects and make sense of their movements and patterns of behavior. We make predictions based on what we've seen (and heard), and we note whether our predictions are fulfilled or not. We can put into words what we encounter on screen, as the prisoners do when they argue over what they see and hear, because the experience is itself, for the most part, intelligible and coherent.

In the allegory of the cave, what appear to the prisoners are shadows, and shadows are, precisely, light in the process of being obstructed. There would only be a formless darkness except where there is also light. It is by considering the shadows' structure that they can attend to what surrounds them and makes them possible. The intelligibility of cinema, which we've compared to the projector's light, is not itself one of the elements on screen. It is, however, necessary for the presentation to take place. As light makes things visible but isn't, strictly, seen, the cinematic light signifies those conditions presupposed by any cinematic presentation, as well as those which, evolving in the course of cinema's history, come to serve as presuppositions which make possible new forms of significance on screen. It is, we might say, the invisible structure that makes structured elements visible. We can, instead of focusing on what appears in this or that film, call attention to this structure and consider its impact. At the same time, this structure is meaningless apart from specific presentations, and specific films. Just as shadows would be formless in the absence of the light, the light would illuminate nothing in the absence of the shadows.

A range of dimensions belongs to the conditions of cinematic intelligibility, here compared with the projector's light. There are, at most basic, conditions that belong to any experience whatsoever, such as that to notice anything requires it have a determinate shape and at least salient qualities we are capable of discerning and following as it moves and changes. To identify things on screen as what they are requires, further, that they exhibit at least some of the properties that allow us to pick out such things in everyday life. The presentation of different kinds of things presupposes our anticipation of dimensions obscured in that presentation – as, for example, the fact that to see a door is to expect there's something beyond it, and that even where the screen itself is flat, the opening of the door will make possible the passing through it of something visible.

There are, further, conventions belonging to cinema. One such convention is the cinematic frame, which we understand to mark the difference between the film's presentation of a world apart and the world we inhabit, of which the film experience forms merely a part. As we noted in connection with *A Clockwork Orange*, the frame at once marks off a segment of the world it presents or represents, and marks off that world as distinct from the world into which it is projected, from the apparatus that projects it, and from the audience that accepts it. At the same time, there are elements of cinema that complicate this distinction, or that call it into question, as when a face on screen appears to look us in the eye or when a voice proceeding from the screen addresses the audience or when elements on screen appear to refer to the apparatus responsible for the film itself. In this case, we have an image that shows itself to be an image, a shadow that shows itself to be a shadow and thereby provokes those, enthralled by the shadows, to reflect upon their workings.

There are conventions of cinema that, by the uses to which they are put, come to mean more and imply more than they had before, and this expansion of the possibilities of significance, of what it means to see a face or hear a voice on screen or see a flashback or hear music, for example, can be presupposed by later filmmakers. The jump cut, for example, in which a brief segment of a visibly continuous action is interrupted by an apparently unmotivated and jarring edit, was made famous in Jean-Luc Godard's film *Breathless*; at the time it seemed to be (and might well have been) a mistake, or an irreverent rejection of cinematic standards. Now it hardly surprises at all, and suggests almost directly a vitality or spontaneity in the scene on screen, or, in another context, an urgency in action. The twentieth-century French philosopher Gilles Deleuze notes in his volumes on *Cinema* that whereas most films made before World War II presented elements to be understood by audiences as belonging to a coherent spatio-temporal reality, some innovative filmmakers after – such as Alain Resnais – began to create works presenting a world fragmented into multiple and competing sheets of time. They sometimes present incompatible events, in times that overlap, for example. Their films tend to be irreducible to a single, coherent narrative, in which we can say what took place first and next and after. Alternatively, some films unfold within their own, real, lived sense of time, whose ebb and flow is irreducible to generic clocktime and threatens to supplant for its duration the audience's experience of time. Even where such films tell stories that defy audience expectations for meaning and coherence, they are on the whole accepted as having something important to say. Their fragmentation of narrative significance is itself taken to be significant, because their emergence coincided historically with a widespread and growing suspicion of narratives that adopt privileged points of view or that pretend to make sense of everything at once.

When philosophers talk about film, they often focus on just the most obvious of the elements that together make up and make possible the film experience, the film itself. They talk about images, about story, about characters and points of view; they talk (less frequently) about techniques, and they consider their implications for thinking about the subjects that philosophers like to talk about. A lesson to learn about film by comparing it with Plato's allegory is that the film experience as a whole is what is responsible for the significance we draw from this or that movie. We can abstract from this whole, and focus on the film itself, its content, and the issues it suggests, or we can consider the apparatus, the technology and techniques and the industry, or we can think about the director and the stylistic and thematic preoccupations that bind together a body of work, or we can reflect upon the cultural conditions of the spectator, or upon the cognitive powers called upon by audiences making sense of what they see. To focus on the film only is to make the same mistake as the prisoners in Plato's cave, unaware that the realities they encounter are conditioned. There is another possibility, which doesn't exclude any of these various considerations but which gives them focus around the question how these components contribute to the making of cinematic meaning or intelligibility.

This other possibility is to reflect upon the light that links these components together, to reflect upon the conditions for cinematic intelligibility, what makes it possible that we make sense of cinema at all, and what are the distinctive ways of making sense revealed through cinema. We can, at the same time, reflect upon what these conditions for cinematic intelligibility, and their ways of being worked out in specific films, have to teach us about how we make sense of anything at all. Another, simpler, way to put this is to say that we can set aside facts and thoughts about the film itself, about the history of production and technologies that bring it to the screen, and about the audience and their cultural baggage, and we can focus on the experience of the film, on the film's ways of making sense to its audience. On the present reading of the allegory of the cave, philosophy is not so much an escape from the conditions of everyday life as it is a transformation of the experience of everyday life, a transformation that comes from reflecting on the light itself rather than exclusively upon what it reveals. Film's philosophy, likewise, does not treat film as merely an illustration to be left behind for the abstract and technical work of philosophical abstraction. Film-philosophy amounts rather to a new way of looking at film on its own terms, as a complex social phenomenon that generates experience and meaning, and also provokes questions that can put it into dialogue with philosophical reflections about the intelligible forms embedded in everyday life.

The allegory of the cave does more than offer a rich comparison with cinema. Like many of the images and myths that Plato has Socrates describe throughout his dialogues, it is an image that has the potential to elevate its audience upwards on the divided line. To reflect on its significance is to reconsider the nature of human experience, and to begin to consider the ideas upon which experience depends. Cinema's richest imagery has the same potential. The image of Alex, for example, strapped inside a theater, eyes pried open and compelled to witness cinematic imitations of his very own actions, is among the most potent in a film filled with striking imagery. By depicting in extremity the condition of the cinematic spectator, it provokes us to consider just what happens to us at the movies.

3   Feeling and image
The Ludovico Technique

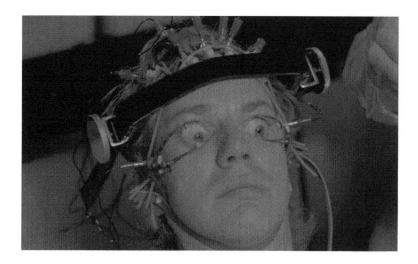

We started out with his face. He was cunning and dangerous, assured of his power. He looked us in the eye, challenged us to look away, and began to tell his story. We return now to the same face, now powerless, no longer confident of his capacity to master whatever he sees either through intimidation and violence or with his boyish charm. He's no longer looking at us, but, like us, at a screen. Rendered passive by an apparatus that secures his body and holds his eyes wide open, he's forced to witness moving images that aren't so different from some we'd already seen of his exploits prior to incarceration. If, in the beginning, we saw ourselves seen, this image might be thought to depict the condition of seeing what we can do nothing about. We should consider at least the extent to which this condition resembles our own as we watch this (or any) film.

He'd been imprisoned for murder, sentenced to fourteen years. After serving two, Alex managed to get himself selected for an experimental program aimed at rehabilitating criminals. Developed by scientist Dr Brodsky, the project was sponsored by the government as part of a political strategy promising a radical new approach to crime. Their aim is to force criminals to conform, by means of a technology that generates an aversion to behaviors the government rejects. Released from jail and into the custody of scientists, he's given a nice meal and "vitamins" from a vial marked "Exp. Serum No. 114." He's brought to an unusual theater, where he is seated alone, with the scientists observing from behind, as a technician prepares him for his first treatment.

Rape and spectatorship

Alex's situation here resembles that of the prisoners in Plato's allegory in several ways. He's bound in a straitjacket, eyelids locked open, unable to look away from the images before his eyes. There are scientists behind him, who aren't marching, but are at least responsible for this procession of images, and for the sounds that seem to proceed from the screen. Alex reacts to the images by making associations, by relating what he sees to what he's seen before, and wondering what will come next. While there aren't other prisoners with him, he can and does talk about his reactions with Drs Brodsky and Branom. There are, though, important differences. He is bound to his chair, but volunteered to be there. He wasn't born in this condition, and can compare what he sees on screen both with other motion pictures and with what he's encountered elsewhere. In that sense, he resembles us, the willing witnesses of his story. He might be thought to resemble us later, as well, when his initial fascination with the images on screen turns into or mingles with disgust and he wants to look away, but something compels him to continue watching until the end.

We still hear his voice, and the voice is the same. The voice, now secure, presents what we are seeing as something that has already happened, over and done with, and describes the Alex we see as a "cooperative young malchik." He's not a victim, helpless, in a chair, but merely "putting up" with much discomfort for the sake of his release from prison. After describing the theater and the setup, he settles in, satisfied, to watch some films. He'd told Dr Branom, who'd given him a shot that morning and explained that watching movies would be part of his treatment, that he liked "to viddy the old films now and again." When the first one starts up, he becomes something of a film critic, noting with appreciation that it "was a very good professional piece of cine, like it was done in Hollywood." He notes how realistic are the screams and moans of the victim, and the heavy breathing of the perpetrators.

We have to take his word for it. We barely hear these sounds – apart from the sharp thwap of repeated blows to the victim's head – above the din of an increasingly chaotic electronic musical soundtrack. We do see at least a part of the film. Four young men, dressed up very much like Alex and his former companions, punch and slap an older man in a suit, and after he stumbles down a stairwell they hold him up against a pillar, beating him repeatedly. It's shot handheld and shaky, unlike much of the film we'd been watching to this point; apart, that is, from the more subjective sequences during the assault and rape of the writer's wife. If we don't hear the sounds that Alex describes as "realistic" – and even if we consider that the sounds we do hear, the music and the blows alike, sound highly stylized, artificial – still, the sequence looks real enough, as real as anything we've seen so far, and more so than most of it. The unsteady movement of the camera makes the action feel unplanned and spontaneous, as if life captured unaware. It contrasts sharply with the highly stylized presentations of violence that seem to favor Alex's view of himself, and contrasts as well with the stable wide and tight framings of Alex now, a captive audience in the otherwise empty theater.

His feelings at first are vicarious thrills. As he explains later to his doctor, he always "used to feel real horrorshow" whether doing or watching violence. His reaction, then, on this occasion, clearly strikes him as odd. At first, he considers that his stomach was upset by his breakfast, but well into the second film he becomes awfully nauseous. His enjoyment of the onscreen entertainment dims as he sickens, and the frame depicts his confusion. Alternating between showing us what he sees – a young woman being raped repeatedly – and his face as he sees it, we see that while at first aroused and fascinated he is gradually becoming more disgusted as he watches. We don't hear what he hears, but the soundtrack mirrors his feelings for us. In other scenes we've examined, the joyfulness and harmony of the music stood in stark contrast with our likely response to the violence on screen, but nevertheless gave a sense of his own exuberant reactions. Now the increasingly ominous tones suggest a likely affinity between the emotional state we see on his face and our own response to the behavior we witness along with him. We see his eyelids straining, and deep distorted tones emanate from the screen as his voice describes his desperate efforts to shut his eyes or look away. He has begun to associate the feeling in his body with what he's seeing on screen, rather than with the meal he ate before. He imagines now that closing or averting his eyes would alleviate the pain. As he begs to be released, Dr Brodsky behind him points out to his fellow scientists that he is now beginning to make rewarding associations between the drug-induced "deep feelings of terror and helplessness" and his own reaction to the violence he sees on screen.

His condition as he views the gang rape recalls that of the writer, also compelled to look on as his wife was assaulted sexually by Alex and his droogs. They'd secured the writer's arms and legs with tape and held his body immobile, directing his face toward his wife as Alex prepared for the violent finale of his song-and-dance routine. "Viddy well," Alex had insisted, twice, commanding the helpless writer to observe the whole performance. Now, however, it is Alex bound and forced to watch, eyes secured wide open as an assistant delivers eye drops to maintain clarity of sight. What he sees, likewise, is a group of leering, longhaired, young men dressed up in black hats, white shirts and pants, just like the gang Alex had commanded, but in this case unmasked. Four of them pin a young woman to the grass, while another lies on top of her, groping and thrusting, as two more stand beside them, their enthusiastic witnesses. Both Alex and the writer are unable to look away, both sickened as they watch, even if for very different reasons. In each case, though, the film highlights more the pain registered in the spectator's eyes and face than the trauma of the victims, suggesting that the enforced passivity of looking is itself a kind of violation, a violent visual assault that they are powerless to prevent. The comparison of forced seeing with rape is accentuated in both instances by a phallic object brought close to the eyes of the spectator. In the case of the writer, as we've noted, it is Alex's fake proboscis that juts erect toward his eyeballs. In the case of Alex it is a much more modest phallus: an eyedropper moving in and out of the close-up and from eye-to-eye, dripping fluids to ensure that his "glassies" remain moist, as his eyes are pried open and he is unable to blink. There was another phallus, as well, that was ultimately responsible for Alex's adverse reaction to the images he witnessed. In the previous scene, Alex was asked to roll over on his side, lift up his gown, and the nurse penetrated his posterior with drugs injected through a long and sharp hypodermic needle.

The blunt comparison between Alex and the writer, on the one hand, and between the condition of each and that of the victims they witness, on the other, hints also at our own condition as spectators to these very images, as we watch them violated as they witness violation. Unlike them, we aren't held down, and we come to the theater by choice, but in that sense we are similar to Alex, who elected to undergo the experimental treatment without knowing what to expect. Even the writer, reluctantly, asked his wife to open the door to Alex, thus inviting in their assailants, in spite of some suspicions. Of course, by comparison, a rape is still a rape if the victim flirts with strangers, or knows the rapists, and even if she invites them into her home. The key difference seems to be that we at least can always walk away, in spite of any social or other pressures we feel compelling us to stay. Still, we can be taken by surprise and shocked, and even feel violated by what we see on screen, and we can't say in advance what the impact of any given film might be. While we can choose to avoid this or that film, or walk out when it is uncomfortable, it is hard to avoid completely the images that surround us. In the world of *A Clockwork Orange*, for example, there's hardly a wall outside without some obscene graffiti, or indoors without provocative paintings or photographs. In fact the real world's hardly different, and even where the imagery is not directly sexual it is still aimed largely to channel or draw upon our desires and impulses, with the intention of provoking specific reactions without our explicit consent. Television and social media, for example, which seem aimed at entertaining audiences, exist, arguably, and above all, to provide eyeballs to advertisers.

What are we to make of the film's visual suggestion that images can inflict a kind of rape, a violent sexual assault upon unwilling or reluctant eyes? To see this as anything more than an irresponsible metaphor requires reflection on the meaning of the term. Rape is usually defined as sexual assault, widely understood as nonconsensual sexual penetration. That images can impact their viewer sexually is demonstrated by pornography, but while the forced viewing of violent sexual images is, by definition, nonconsensual and sexual, the penetration in such instances is metaphorical rather than literal. While there's no room in a legal definition of rape for metaphor – and in a legal context it remains notoriously difficult to prove anything but penetration – it is nevertheless clear that "assault" leaves room for a range of activities beyond physical penetration.

Defined in relation to sex, rape is clearly not just about it. Even sex is not just about sex, it's about intimacy, about opening up to the other, allowing oneself to be touched and affected, both bodily and in one's cares. We are sexual beings insofar as what we desire in the other is the desire of the other, and rape involves precisely the refusal to allow the desires of the other to have bearing on one's actions. The sexual act, intercourse, is special just because it puts lovers in a situation where they are utterly vulnerable, where they, literally, open themselves up to each other, trusting each other to take only what is freely given, and to give freely only what is desired. It is, therefore, fraught with enormous risk, and, for a variety of reasons, many are afraid or unwilling to render themselves vulnerable in the way that honest sex demands. Alex, for example, displays little interest in it. His rape is a performance, a display of what he takes to be his artistry, and afterwards he has self-aggrandizing fantasies while he listens to his music and satisfies himself physically, alone in his bedroom.

Where sex involves fantasy – as it always does to some degree – it is its sharing, its reciprocity, that expands the boundaries of one's privacy beyond the limits of one's bedroom and one's head. In this, there is, in addition to risk, the possibility of reward, of the discovery about oneself what one cannot see or feel by oneself alone. We, usually, think fulfillment is a matter of getting what we want, of satisfying desires. Yet our desires are, for the most part, shaped by influences we never chose, and to fulfill them is, often, either to be driven to act on impulses we can't help or to fulfill interests of the institutions that inform us without our explicit consent. We come of age and into desires we hardly understand. It is in the erotic bond and in bonds of friendship, when what we desire is the desire of another, a desire that transcends the limits of our own, that we begin to forge with our friends and lovers what it is we want and want to be for one another, and in the process catch a glimpse of who we are and just might be ourselves. A lesson from another great Platonic text, *The Symposium*, is that sex is, at its very best, a form of dialogue. It is a dialogue in which we at once encounter our own limits, and the limits of our erotic bonds, and are challenged to transcend them in the course of conversation, intercourse, with others who see differently. This is something Alex can't conceive and wants no part of.

The next day Alex does encounter two young women in a record shop and invite them home for sex – but what is notable is that the film speeds through it to the tune of Rossini's *William Tell* overture as Alex undresses and couples first with one, then both, then another, and as he finishes with the one he is ready once again for the other. So even though this sex is consensual, for him it's just another performance, in which he puts on display his sexual prowess. He invites them over on the pretense of showing them his stereo, and including the story in his narrative to us is, effectively, no more than a chance to show off additional equipment. Sex, throughout the film, is depicted as a kind of performance or demonstration, intended for an audience, rather than a scene of intimate sharing. Alex, at least, is shown to be incapable of that.

If we wish – and it makes sense – to preserve the term "rape" for those sexual assaults involving physical penetration, it is nevertheless clear that other forms of sexual assault are akin to and can be no less devastating for the victim than actual rape. The young woman released inadvertently when Alex and his droogs came upon Billy Boy on the stage, for example, was never actually penetrated but certainly was violated by the young thugs wearing Nazi military gear who tore off her clothing and dragged her, struggling, over to a dirty mattress. Consider, further, that rape victims who are compelled to recount their experience in court, and who may be vilified in the media or by the defense team in order to minimize their credibility, often describe the experience as a "second rape." In some cases, at least, for its violent impact on the victim, this seems more than merely metaphor. At the very least, it can be a kind of assault, where the sense of violation is real.

The question is whether it can be more than merely a metaphor for what happens to the spectator. Consider first the case of Alex and the writer. What they both see – an assault – upsets them, and they want to make it stop but can't. It makes them feel sick, and its impact is lasting and for both outwardly similar. The nausea displayed on the writer's face, later, when he realizes it is Alex in his bathtub, is quite like the sickened look on Alex's face when he contemplates violence following treatment. Their experience, then, affects not only their thoughts but, we might say, penetrates into or inscribes itself onto their bodies – it is traumatic, a devastating memory that shapes how they relate and respond to events in the world, and not merely how they think of them. In the case of Alex, as we see, his thoughts are overwhelmed by feelings of sickness; even the writer, who intends to use Alex for political gain, has these thoughts overcome by a palpable reaction when he hears Alex singing, which doubles him over and turns his face a sickened red. Even later, as he offers Alex a glass of wine while they wait for his friends to arrive, we see that he's lost control almost completely of his bodily reactions, as he is unable to compose himself, unable to speak without blurting things out unnaturally. The difference, in part at least, seems to be that the rape the writer sees is real, involving someone whom he cares about, and what Alex sees is representation, a mere fiction. Alex does wonder, for a moment, in the novel at least, whether the rape he sees on screen is real, and then convinces himself it can't be by reflecting that the actors wouldn't agree and the state would not have asked them. Even so, it is not quite right to say that one witnesses reality and the other merely fiction, since what both witnessed was a fabrication, created for us by Kubrick and his creative team. Kubrick's decision to omit Alex's musings on whether what he witnessed was real – it was even included in the screenplay but not the finished film – may have been intended to provoke in us the question just how essential is the difference.

The difference between a real, recorded, rape and one merely simulated for the camera is, to be sure, decisive in its impact on the participants, who are actors playing a role in the one case and rapists and victims in the other. The question is what difference it makes to a spectator who, presumably, can't discern the difference. The writer, presumably, can. We – who as audiences accustomed to the conventions of cinema presumably also know that what we see is being faked – are meant to imagine or suppose that what he sees is real, and that what Alex sees during treatment is a fictional representation. In the case of Alex, though, it wouldn't likely make much of a difference had he thought that it was real. He was, after all, responsible for the real rape the writer had witnessed. In the scene where that took place, as discussed above, the film depicts something of the difference between Alex's stylized narration of the event – which is to say, his imaginary depiction of it as its instigator – and the experience of the Alexanders, who felt its visceral impact directly. The impact on him, now, of these images while in treatment, is due to the very real effect of the drugs they injected into him. For typical audiences of the film, though, it is likely to make a very real difference that we know it isn't real, that it is merely represented.

Some film theorists such as Jean-Louis Baudry – notably inspired by considerations of the link between Plato's cave and cinema – considered that the very apparatus of cinema rendered moviegoers passive, forcing an identification with the position of the camera, and subjecting them as subjects to enthrallment by its imagery. The effect of cinema upon its audiences, he argued, is like that of dreams, which might be said to operate at a level below that of critical thinking, with the result that their impact upon us, their power to shape attitudes and values, is something greater than that of ordinary reality. If so, and assuming an audience resistant to being affected in this way, this might legitimately be compared to a kind of violation. Still, though we are certainly moved by movies, and feel powerfully the impact of the scenes on screen, we are nevertheless not (usually) moved by them to respond to what takes place there. The clearest reason for this seems to be that while our feelings are affected by the likeness, our actions are tempered by the awareness that what we're watching isn't real. We do not, in other words, lose our critical capacities when the lights dim in the cinema. We are passive by choice, we are active in thought. We may very well be impacted viscerally by disturbing images we witness, but remain unlike either Alex or the writer, whose passivity is forced.

Consider yet another contrast with another kind of spectator, present at a real act such as rape, and not rendered powerless by those present, but remaining inactive by choice. The two thugs, for example, in the film that Alex watches, are neither actively holding the young woman down nor actually raping her, but seem enthusiastic at the prospect. We might also consider the audience of Alex's post-treatment demonstration to the public after treatment, which looks on in interest and satisfaction as he's forced to lick an aggressor's shoe. Or, if Alex and his droogs had chosen to wait in the shadows a bit longer before interrupting Billy Boy and friends in the act, enjoying the show, as it were, that played out on stage of the derelict casino, their mode of spectatorship would clearly constitute a kind of participation. It is a way of being present and aware of an unfolding situation, treating it merely as something to be looked at and accepted, rather than responded to.

Not everyone present in a situation is able to intervene or respond appropriately. Even those who aren't forced to be inactive, like the writer, may be paralyzed by fear or may rightly recognize that to intervene would be both futile and dangerous. There is, though, a key difference between merely looking on, whether for enjoyment or curiosity, and what might be called a critical witnessing. Prior to his mounting sickness, Alex was watching eagerly. Grinning at the beginning of the first film, he says he attempted to ignore his illness in order to concentrate on the next. Mr Alexander, the writer, by contrast, doesn't watch his wife's rape from either curiosity or lust. In fact, it seems, he doesn't want to watch at all, and still he chooses to in order to stand as witness. While he is held down, his eyes aren't forced open. He seems in fact to force them open himself in spite of an inclination to shut them. We see his eyebrows raised unnaturally, as he blinks involuntarily. He might have given in, and closed his eyes or let them drift – or merely watched, accepting he could do nothing. Whether out of shock or in outrage, he was unable to accept that. There was at least one option that remained for him: he could witness the horror, so that he later could bear witness.

The manifest tension displayed on the writer's face as he was held down watching Alex might remind readers of Plato's *Republic*, of a pivotal scene in which Socrates aims to show that we are driven, in our actions, by distinctly directed and often contradictory aims and impulses. He describes a man, Leontius, who was walking outside of the walls of Athens when he noticed the corpses of recently executed men upon the ground. He found the sight repulsive and considered it shameful to stare, and yet something in him – curiosity? lust? – compelled him to look. Overcome by this desire, he ran toward the corpses, held his eyes open wide and berated them in disgust, "Look, you damned wretches, take your fill of the fair sight" (440a). There is tension in our souls. We have multiple wants and aspirations, and in this case it was desire that overcame the sense of dignity or pride that is averse to engaging in dishonorable acts. It seems to be a related tension that the scientists aim to generate in Alex, who appears unashamed by his lusts. He enjoys looking at violence and debauchery, and the scientists aim to generate an artificial disgust in him by means of their technique.

In the case of the writer, by contrast, it seems to be his sense of care combined with a desire for justice that compels him to look even as he desires to shut his eyes. Things are different when, after spending time in prison, Alex returns inadvertently to the writer's house seeking shelter. At first, the writer welcomes him in and cares for him, considering him a victim of the government's unjust approach to crime. Later, however, when the writer realizes that Alex is the man who raped his wife and put him in a wheelchair, he allows his rage and desire for revenge to overcome his plan to score political points against the opposition while rectifying what he considered to be the injustice of Alex's treatment. The trauma of witnessing can be a shock to thought, which is felt in the body, an assault on the way one sees the world, which can easily upset all prior considerations. It is impossible to say in advance what the impact will be: whether it will lead to incapacity or to a paralyzing fear, anxiety, or hatred, or whether it will become an impetus to reflection or a critical response.

What makes the difference between merely looking on passively – however one may be affected, whether with enjoyment or boredom, arousal or fear – on the one hand, and an active witnessing, on the other, seems to be something in the quality of awareness. In the one case, the object of vision is treated as something whose significance is already given, as something that simply is what it appears to be. How one then relates to it depends on one's attitudes and dispositions. In the case of critical witnessing, the viewer refuses (or is unable) to accept the status of a mere spectator, and stands instead in judgment, insisting that the meaning and importance of what is seen is something that calls for an assessment and response. It is to treat the truth of what is seen not merely as what it appears to mean and be, but as something that's in question. It is, in other words, akin to making the turn that Plato identifies with philosophy in the allegory of the cave.

Consider how Alex describes what he witnesses. Ignoring his sickness he tried to concentrate on the second film, which "jumped right away on a young devotchka, who was being given the old in-out, in-out, first by one malchick, then another, then another." As a visual description, it is accurate enough, but it doesn't really get at what is really going on. To say it is a gang rape gets much closer, because to use the term knowingly is to acknowledge an injustice, to assert a violation. One can, surely, use the word without thinking it is wrong – and Alex might as well have said it when it is clear he isn't troubled – but to see it *as* a rape is to see it as a wrong, which means to think it in relation to a standard that isn't simply private. It may also mean to intervene, but even where that isn't possible it is at least a provocation to a critical moral judgment. Whether one follows up on that sense, whether one considers, as we have briefly, just what is wrong about it, and examines, for example, just how it is that representations of rape serve to shape public awareness of gender and power, is a separate matter. There is no guarantee that a witness in this sense will inquire further, and give expression or bear witness to the significance discovered. To see it, though, as more than what it merely appears to be, and as standing in relation to ideas and institutions that go beyond it and nevertheless shape our perception of it, is to catch sight of the beginnings of real thinking. It is to illuminate the shadows, transform them into thought – to pursue a shadow philosophy.

Music and morality

To compare this scene further with Plato's allegory, we might note that while Alex doesn't take his situation as a provocation to philosophical thinking, he does, like the released prisoner, also undergo a kind of forced education. Effectively in chains, he is, paradoxically, like the one who is dragged about. He is being educated, but not with a Socratic education that takes place through dialogue, with his assumptions spelled out and examined for consistency. Rather than be forced from the cave by being led to consider the ideas underlying his opinions, he is held fast in his chair and compelled to feel differently about them. He is dragged by being drugged, educated chemically. It is an education by way of feelings and associations, meant to reform his dispositions, rather than change his mind. As Dr Branom tells him, the associations he's making while bound and watching movies are meant to restore him to a condition of health. "Of course it was horrible," she tells him. "Violence is a very horrible thing, that's what you're learning now. Your body is learning it." According to the doctors, it is not enough to know what is right. One has to feel it. The body, rather than the mind, is the locus of their teaching.

Their attitudes on this become clearer the next day, when Alex arrives for another session. This time he's watching images of Nazi soldiers and symbols, of mass destruction and war, what he describes as "nasty bits of ultraviolence." This time, though, the soundtrack is different, there's no violence on the soundtrack itself, just music. He becomes aware of the accompanying music, from his beloved Beethoven's Ninth Symphony, and begs them to stop: "it's a sin, it's a sin, it's a sin." "What's all this about sin?" asks Dr Brodsky, perplexed.

What, precisely, does he consider here a sin? "Using Ludwig Van like that," cries Alex, "he's done no harm to anyone, Beethoven just wrote music." What is unclear is how using his music in any way harms Beethoven. Alex talks as if the music and composer are linked, that the scientists are "using Ludwig Van" when they're using his music, that they're doing him harm when they misuse his compositions. We often do refer to works by the name of their creator. We speak of "a Picasso" or of playing Mozart or Beethoven or the Beatles. This is, usually, shorthand for "a painting by Picasso" or a composition or song by the rest. Still, his mention that Beethoven himself did nothing wrong as a reason it's a sin suggests the link for him is more direct. Misusing art is a crime against the artist.

Unless he's just inconsistent, applying different standards to himself and to others, he can't consider it wrong generally, and a wrong against musicians, to link their music with violence. We could, in that case, level the same accusation against him and against Kubrick for their choice of classics to accompany mayhem. There is, perhaps, the difference that in this case the feeling's all wrong. The music's meant to elevate. He's supposed to feel triumphant, ecstatic, delighted, and the music and the mayhem combine to give him those emotions. In this case, though, what he's feeling doesn't click. He should be feeling ecstatic but is instead horrendously sick. The trick is that for the audience, at least, when we're watching the film, the images and music also work against one another. We feel disgust for what we see, and yet the music is uplifting. The very thing he considers a sin is deliberately done to us, but for us it provokes the question of the role music can and should play in connection with moving images.

The sin, perhaps, of the scientists is that they had never even considered the question. They had made the link in ignorance. From their reaction to his outburst it is clear they had no inkling of his obsession and no intention of creating this specific aversion; for both it is merely a piece of music, as suitable as any for a "background score." In any case they claim it can't be helped, it's too late now to change the program. Dr Brodsky's casual response that it can't be helped, that it is, perhaps, an appropriate element of punishment that should please the prison governor, betrays that he cares very little about the moral implications of their experiment, and much less for its aesthetics. What matters to the scientists – as to the Minister, as he explains in response to the Chaplain's objections – is only whether or not it works. This flies in the face of the justification for the procedure that the Minister of the Interior himself delivers: that it is a new approach to crime that avoids the hypocrisy of punishment. The doctor's lack of interest in the question, and unconcern with the possible moral implications of their project, shouldn't blind us to the possibility there is something serious at stake in the selection of a background score.

Desperate, screaming, Alex claims to be cured – "praise God!" he cries, he's learned his lesson, sees now that what he's done is wrong. "It's wrong because it's, like, against society. It's wrong because everyone has the right to live and be happy without being tolchoked and knived." While his words make a strong, quick case against anti-social behavior, Dr Brodsky sees directly through his ruse. "You're not cured yet boy … you must really leave it to us." It's not enough, according to the doctors, to know, or be able to state, the reasons why it is wrong. One has to feel them. Conversation and argument alone, then, are inadequate to cure the criminal. True education, on their account, involves more than adopting new ideas. It is not enough to change one's mind; one has to have a change of heart. In Alex's case, it is a change in the gut, which comes in the form of a desire to vomit.

Following his treatment, the Minister presents Alex on yet another stage before an audience of media representatives and dignitaries. An abusive older man and a lovely naked woman approach Alex in sequence, and he's helpless to respond either in anger or in lust without becoming violently sick. "You see ladies and gentlemen," the Minister speaks to the assembly, after congratulating Alex, placing his hand on his shoulder, both facing the spotlight, "our subject is impelled toward the good, by, paradoxically, being impelled toward evil. The intention to act violently is accompanied by strong feelings of physical distress. To counter these, the subject has to switch to a diametrically opposed attitude." The treatment, then, demanded that Alex associate his drug-induced physiological state with the attitudes and inclinations generated within him by the films he was witnessing.

It is, of course, not enough for him to be disgusted by this or that film, or even this or that act – whether rape or attack. It would also not serve the purpose for him to associate his state of terror and helplessness with being seated in this specific theater or in the presence of that doctor. It is not enough for him to become sick while watching others rape and attack. He has to associate these feelings with his own desire to commit acts of violence, and then his desire to avoid the pain associated with these feelings has to be stronger than his desire for the pleasures of sex and the excitement of violence. What this seems to require is that he identify with the perpetrators of violence in the films he's watching, so that he is not merely associating disgust with the thrill of watching others commit crimes, but with his own intentions to behave badly. It is easy to see how this might happen in the case of the first two films, since the beating of the older man and the rape of the young woman are done by young men dressed up and behaving just like Alex and his droogs, albeit lacking in panache. We've already seen throughout the film that Alex is adept at imagining himself involved in violent acts of others.

The inclusion of war footage the second day is more puzzling. Is he supposed to be disgusted by fascism, by patriotic assemblies, by Nazis, by war and destruction generally? It is hard to say exactly what the scientists may have hoped for, since the upshot might as easily have been to put Alex off from ever watching the news or from enlisting in the army. A clue to its significance for the film as a whole comes from the inclusion of footage from Leni Riefenstahl's *Triumph of the Will*, a formally brilliant propaganda documentary designed to celebrate the successes of Hitler and of Nazi Germany.

Aesthetically, it's a triumph, the work of an artist at the height of her craft. Morally and politically, it's repugnant, a celebration of fascism that appears completely to ignore the interests of its victims. In that sense, it resembles a number of scenes throughout *A Clockwork Orange*, where acts of violence are depicted as if they were performance artworks, improvised by Alex.

The inclusion of Beethoven, a signature of Alex's style, may have been an accident from the point of view of the scientists, but suggests that the impact of this presentation is to undermine his aesthetics, his sense of theater and showmanship, and to make his taste for musically heightened violence unpalatable. It is, perhaps, this that he objects to, and considers a "sin": not the fact that Beethoven is employed to glorify Nazis (Riefenstahl used Wagner and German folk music in her own score), but rather that the association of this music with triumphant violence, and, more generally, the celebration of aesthetic over moral and political values, is itself rendered repugnant.

The association of Beethoven's symphony with images of fascist marches and war footage, accentuated in the film by the fact that a Nazi swastika fills the screen just at the moment when Alex recognizes the music, has a further implication. Music, out of context, can be considered morally and politically neutral. It is the uses to which it is put, to generate feelings associated with ideas or provoke dispositions to action, which make the moral and political difference. The fact that Alex is cultured, that he appreciates fine classical music, and has a taste for art, has no bearing upon his moral character, or upon his sympathies for fellow human beings. Even Nazis who were responsible for atrocities could and did appreciate Beethoven and other fine arts. At the same time, music has the power to generate and amplify feelings, and can create associations that may either undermine or elevate a natural or prejudicial response to a situation. It is this power that filmmakers generally draw upon in order to heighten or manipulate the emotional state of the audience, during a love scene, or a battle, or a moment of familial reconciliation. It is this power that Alex draws upon as if it were his drug-laced milk, to sharpen himself up for a bit of ultraviolence, and that Kubrick employs in his depictions of Alex's actions to undermine or complicate our natural reactions.

If the proper moral response is not guaranteed by having the right ideas, but requires, as Plato's most famous pupil Aristotle would insist, that one be pained and pleased by the right things, then we might consider music indispensable to moral education. Plato thought so, or at least has his teacher Socrates claim in the *Republic*, that for the guardians of the good city it is their early education in music that is above all critical for their moral development. He argued that certain kinds of music could bolster courage where appropriate, and others encourage calm deliberation. Other kinds of music, aimed at excitement without outlet, should be banned from the ideal city. Training in the right kinds of rhythms and harmonies would develop gracefulness and discernment, such that a young guardian would learn to "praise the fine things [and] ... blame and hate the ugly in the right way while he's still young, before he's able to grasp reasonable speech" (*Republic*, 401e). Even if, then, music is morally neutral in the sense that it can be associated with good or bad actions, it still influences attitudes and dispositions, and in that case creating the right associations between music and action can make a significant moral difference.

The difference it makes seems to be precisely its influence on emotional response. An image of, say, a face, like the one that opens up *A Clockwork Orange*, is the same image whether or not it is accompanied by music. Still, the ominous tones that open the film, from Wendy Carlos's electronically synthesized adaptation of Purcell's Music for the Funeral of Queen Mary, set the stage for our assessment of its sinister gaze. An upbeat or pop musical score to open with might have led us to expect a comedy, and would have emphasized the irony in Alex's smile, perhaps led us to laugh at the costumes and silly codpieces that the droogs all wore. The expectations created by different music might have led us astray, as they do throughout the film, and yet the music would have led us to these expectations naturally. Images are inflected, our emotional response to them directed, by the music that accompanies them.

Emotions, moreover, are inseparably of both mind and body. They are neither merely beliefs, nor merely feelings. They are, we might say, beliefs that we feel. They are, more precisely, dispositions, felt in our bodies, to interpret situations a certain way. Or, equally, they are the bodily feelings that accompany certain characteristic types of interpretation. To feel fear is to interpret a situation as threatening, and at the same time is to tremble, to breathe quickly, and to be easily startled, as if under threat. To feel angry at someone is to interpret his actions as offensive, and to feel one's blood as if boiling as adrenaline prepares for a fight. To feel hope is to interpret a situation as promising something good, and to experience an elevation in one's body, to exhibit a ready smile, to look eagerly onward in anticipation of success. For the most part, emotions show on our faces, setting the stage for interactions with others that corroborate our felt interpretations of how we stand with them. To adopt an angry face and tone, for example, may in fact produce the offense or threat that retrospectively justifies the anger. Music, by engaging our bodies in listening, responding to a rhythm, attending to a harmony, can dispose one to feel specific emotions or moods, and at the same time to react to situations in ways that are appropriate to those emotions.

That music has such power to affect our interpretations of and responses to situations suggests that the conditioning Alex receives is merely a more extreme version of what can happen to all of us, when we watch movies or television, when we listen to the radio or a playlist or the news. What Alex's captors aim to do is create new associations, so that he'll interpret situations as calling for different responses from the ones he tends to give them. Since his natural reaction is to associate violence with triumphant and exuberant music, especially that of the "lovely, lovely Ludwig Van," the so-called "Ludovico technique" works to undermine this association, associating violence with feelings of terror and helplessness. Is it merely coincidence that "Ludovico" is the Latinized variation of "Ludwig"? For us, as audience, the association of joyful or emboldening songs with heinous acts worked to modify our natural reactions, aestheticizing the actions and thereby distancing us from their moral repugnance, making it easier not to look away. For Alex, now in the role of audience member, the association of this very association with his own drug-induced feelings of disgust compels him to wish to look away, and will lead him to avoid situations that would provoke his lust for violence in the future.

It is the moral ambivalence, the apparent valorization of violence through aesthetic presentation and musical association, that audiences objected to most when *A Clockwork Orange* was first screened. It should be clear by now that this ambivalence within the film as a whole does not amount to a straightforward rejection of moral values, or to a moral nihilism, as some have claimed. We will return to this issue in Chapter 5. Still, it is easy to see why some, perhaps youthful and immature, viewers of the film, already disposed toward the kind of behavior that Alex exhibits, might have taken the film as an endorsement of and incitement to a stylized approach to criminal violence. As much as he rejected the idea that art was to blame for the actions it was alleged to inspire, even Stanley Kubrick endorsed the ban on his film in the United Kingdom, following an apparent wave of copycat crimes.

The film thus not only explores the possibility that we are conditioned by images and music, but also in its reception posed this very question. Plato, too, as we have already seen, was concerned by the power of stories, images, and song to shape and redirect moral attitudes and character. In this he pits the illuminating power of philosophy against the obfuscation of truth that can accompany storytelling and images, while leaving room for a defense of their potential. His reflections on this topic have widely been considered to amount to arguments for artistic censorship on the part of the state. A close examination of his reasons as they arise in the course of the *Republic* will pave the way for a reconsideration of both the moral perils and philosophical promise of cinema in general and of *A Clockwork Orange* specifically.

4 Plato's critique of poetry and the peril and promise of cinema

The question that begins the conversation in Plato's *Republic* is what is justice and whether it benefits anyone to be just. Socrates claims it does, that doing the right thing is not only good for others but for oneself as well. His audience, however, is less convinced. Plato's own brothers, Glaucon and Adeimantus, suggest that the majority do right only in fear of punishment, and if they could get away with it they'd act with impunity. Even poets, argues Adeimantus, urge justice only as a matter of prudence, suggesting by way of their stories that to act badly is to run the risk of being caught and punished, whether here or in the afterlife. His claim that the majority opinion on these matters is established under the influence of such stories, told to each of us at an early age, sets the stage for Socrates' subsequent inquiry into the epistemological and moral perils of poetry.

In order to see what is justice, and to determine whether it benefits or harms its possessor, Socrates suggests they consider it on a larger scale. We say of individuals that they are just or unjust, but we can say the same of cities. Investigating the nature and origin of justice in the city, says Socrates, may clarify what it is in relation to the individual. The just city requires defenders, men and women trained up to enforce its laws and guard its citizens. They will do this well only if they're raised the right way. The most important aspect of their education, argues Socrates, would come at a very early age, by way of stories told and music heard. He cautions that in an ideal city, much of the poetry and music that was then popular in Greece would have to be banned.

Imitating art

While some of what he cautions regarding the stories of ancient Greece might be thought to pertain only to that time and place and political climate, and to the specific question of how to raise defenders of the ideal city they imagine, still much of it might be considered relevant today. A glance through the children's section of the local bookstore and the youth channels on television and movies catering to kids suggests that while the media and attitudes have changed, the issues Plato raised remain. The stories children heard then were of heroes and gods, monsters and men; now they wake up and fall asleep to the exploits of superheroes and villains, princesses and prince charmings, undersea invertebrates working deadbeat jobs flipping burgers for a stingy boss, geeks and freaks, talented kids and their clueless parents. Given the amount of time average kids spend watching movies and television and videos on- and offline, it would be remarkable if none of this had any impact on their conception of what matters most, what to strive for, and how to be. Children, now as much as then, become who they are in large part by imitating role models. It is likely truer now than ever that their sense of what to value and whom to emulate is heavily influenced by the stories they hear and witness from a very young age on the screens that surround them. We tend to think of storytelling media quite differently than Plato, who was more concerned with their impact on character than with their value as entertainment. We have allowed ourselves to be persuaded, perhaps too quickly, that his concerns are outmoded and misguided. Movies and television are here to stay, and need no new defenders, but perhaps the case for caution in our consumption needs to be made more strongly, and none has made the case more strongly than Plato.

We might consider, specifically, the case of Alex and of the stories and images he was likely exposed to in his youth. We can't say a lot about specifics from the film alone – and even if we think the book it was inspired by is a source of further information about the Alex we see on screen, it doesn't offer much more to go on. Still, on the basis of the film alone we can gather some insight into his upbringing. His parents are permissive, and easily manipulated by Alex. For the most part, it appears, they leave him alone and let him do as he likes. He seems to skip school regularly, claiming to be sick, and his mother shrugs it off, accepting his excuses. Even if his father suspects he isn't always truthful, he's unwilling or unable to do anything about it. This suggests, at least, a lack of interest or ability on the part of his parents to shape his influences, so that he's been left to fend for himself, to define his own eclectic tastes. He does so, however, in the context of a culture that's suffused with erotic images of women in provocative poses. Even the generic portraits that adorn the walls in his parents' home are of well-endowed women whose look invites a sexual gaze. In these images, women are stripped of their individuality, reduced to sexual objects, the most extreme of which, perhaps, is to be seen in the opening scene in the Korova Milk Bar. Statues of women in sexual poses, milky white and delivering milk from their breasts, serve as furniture and adornment and instruments of satisfaction and arousal. Alex's taste in music is distinctive – and he's something of an audiophile, who idolizes Beethoven and collects cassette recordings of his works – but reflects not so much a musical education as eclecticism. The record store he apparently frequents offers him a wide range of possibilities, and he puts things together however he likes. Beyond sexual imagery and music, Alex is exposed to cinema, likely from all ages, but has a special interest in depictions of sex and violence, as suggested by his appreciation of the first films during treatment. We might suppose such depictions to be ubiquitous and popular, from his suggestion that the films seemed very professional, as if they'd been done in Hollywood. Even if Hollywood films now tend to be subtler, the appeal of sex and violence is a common thread throughout. As filmmaker Jean-Luc Godard pointed out provocatively, all it takes to make a movie is "a girl and a gun."

In fact, one might say, Alex is like a kid with unmediated access to cable and internet, lacking a historical sense and seeing everything on a par with everything else. Everything is available and he is exposed to it all. Pop, porn, contemporary, classics; "mashups" that combine image and sound in ways unpredicted by their original creators; advertisements selling everything with sex – and the only, subtle, difference between the world he inhabits in the film and our own is in the level of subtlety. He's grown up with very little guidance, in a society that apparently, for the most part, gives children free reign to roam the streets as long as they reign it in a bit, and the only order he finds is the order he imposes, whether in his locked bedroom where he controls the decor, or by imposing it on the outside, by beating up a bum, by choreographing violence, or by subjecting real women to the represented objectification that he finds everywhere around him.

Socrates, at least, argues that the tales we tell children and the images they're exposed to shape their souls, molding their attitudes and aspirations from an early age. He insists that "the beginning is the most important part of every work and that this is especially so with anything young and tender." Before any formal training they might receive, the stories they hear from caregivers shape their opinions and values, "for at that stage [their souls are] most plastic, and each thing assimilates itself to the model whose stamp anyone wishes to give to it" (377a–b). For this reason he holds that the first and most important task of education is to reflect critically upon the poetry, stories, and music shared with those children whom we wish to grow up and become responsible for preserving and building upon what is worthwhile in our society.

There's an obvious link here to the allegory of the cave: young children are a captive audience to the songs we sing them and the stories we tell them, or that play endlessly on the screens and speakers that surround them. Later they remain captive willingly, in large part because their desires have been trained. Socrates raises a number of concerns about the captivating power of poetry and music, and comparisons with modern life and the connection with the cave allegory allow us to supplement and clarify the issues he raises.

Socrates' concern is not, as we might consider today, that children be exposed to classical art rather than popular entertainment. He objects as much to the venerable works of Homer and Hesiod as he does to lesser contemporary storytellers and musicians. Consider once again Alex, whose obsession with classical music doesn't affect his penchant for harm. When asked about this infatuation in an interview, Stanley Kubrick pointed out that this aspect of the story "suggests the failure of culture to have any morally refining effect on society. Many top Nazis were cultured and sophisticated men, but it didn't do them, or anyone else, much good" (Ciment, *Kubrick*, p. 163). Plato would agree, at least, that it is not by virtue of being venerable or classic that works of art help to cultivate character. Of course, Kubrick also holds that neither popular nor classical art are likely to do any harm, and Plato on this point is less likely to agree.

His initial concerns regarding the music and stories used to educate the guardians can be divided into issues of content and issues of form. He worries, first, that stories portray divinities as responsible for the bad things that happen to people, leading them to blame immortals or fate for their misfortunes. In Homeric epics, in myth, and in lesser stories derived from these, the gods are said to fight amongst themselves, to deceive human beings and each other, and to take advantage. Socrates worries that even heroes are sometimes represented as cowardly, lascivious, and self-indulgent. Even if, outside of religious upbringings, the stories we tell children now make little reference to divinities (except, perhaps, for Santa Claus and superheroes), the question whether they communicate worthwhile values and provide appropriate role models remains significant. We might disagree on what are worthwhile values and role models – and even Socrates expresses hesitation over the specific guidelines his listeners agree to – but the significance of their influence entails these are questions that can't be ignored.

It was concerns over the moral influence of cinematic content that in the United States encouraged Hollywood's implementation of the

Motion Picture Production Code in the 1930s. Also known as the Hays Code, the Production Code was much more specific in its restrictions than anything we find in the *Republic*. The Hays Code was modified over the years and finally dropped in 1968, to be replaced by an age-based content-rating system implemented by the Motion Picture Association of America. This, combined with recurring media scandals over violent and sexual content in films and television, should at least make clear that the questions Plato raises in the *Republic* are not merely relics of ancient times, no longer of concern or relevance. Certainly, it was related concerns about the likelihood of imitators that led to the banning of *A Clockwork Orange*, with Kubrick's approval, in the country where it was produced.

Of course we might disagree over who gets to decide such questions, and, apart from reserving the right to be scandalized by the decisions of others, most would now hold them to be the prerogative of informed individuals and families. Plato is often accused of advocating censorship in these passages, but the issue he has Socrates raise here is different. He's not interested, anachronistically, in curtailing artistic self-expression or in preventing dissemination of information. The aim, at least in the early parts of the *Republic*, is not so much to silence the free speech of adults, as to enable the free self-development of children. To blame the gods for the evil in one's life is to encourage complacency, to fear death is to enable uncertainty to rule one's choices. Children lack the capacity to choose what materials will shape their values, and by the time they can choose their values have become settled. It is for this reason, and for the fact that parents are pushovers, that advertisers now put so much research and money into appealing to kids. Socrates expresses a related insight when in connection with the allegory of the cave he suggests it isn't enough to cut the chains binding prisoners – they'd need to be dragged out of the cave unwilling. By the time they reach the age of adulthood, they believe in and accept the shadows as their only reality. Likewise, by the time children grow up they largely take for granted certain attitudes and ideas embedded in the images they've consumed.

Plato is writing about what falls under the Greek conception of "music," encompassing the range of creations thought to be inspired by the Muses, including epic poetry, myth, theatrical comedy and tragedy, and, of course, music in the narrow sense. Exactly how and to what extent the content of such things then, as well as the content of cinema and television and other modern media now shape the opinions and values and behaviors of media consumers is an empirical question, to be studied by social scientists. What these values mean, whether they're worthwhile, and what it's like to live through them are, broadly, philosophical questions. Plato notes, though, that ideas and attitudes can be communicated not only by the content of stories and music, but by their form as well. Stories inform their audiences not only by what they say, but by how they say it. Socrates' remarks on the impact of storytelling form round off his initial discussion of the education of the guardians, and he returns to the theme and broadens its scope at the conclusion of the *Republic*. His account of poetic imitation is especially provocative for thinking how art shapes identity, and has an important bearing on distinctive features of cinema.

Socrates urges storytellers and poets to speak in their own voices, narrating situations they describe directly rather than acting out their various parts. That would eliminate at least the theater and dramatic recitations of poetry. Socrates singles out for censure, as well, those who imitate noises of animals and nature, crashing thunder and the like. His remarks would apply, more recently, to most of vaudeville and comedy, radio shows, cinema, and television. Imitating someone or something else, he argues, serves both to distract one from one's proper work and affects one's character negatively. We become what we pretend to be repeatedly. It is notable that the kids in *A Clockwork Orange* – from Alex and his droogs to Billy Boy and his gang – put on costumes and act out roles in an ongoing performance with the city as their stage and other people as their props. It is not just an act, because in fact it shapes who they become, and has impact on those around them. A good person, Socrates says, would be ashamed to imitate just anything, and a child who imitates everything can hardly grow up a good person. "Or haven't you observed that imitations," he asks, "if they are practiced continually from youth onwards, become established as habits and nature, in body and sounds and in thought?" If the city's guardians are to imitate something or someone, it should be appropriate role models, "men who are courageous, moderate, holy, free, and everything of the sort" (395c–d). We might consider, incidentally, that Plato's *Republic*, narrated in the voice of Socrates, allows the author himself to imitate in writing the manner and insights of his own former teacher.

There are notable gaps in the argument, though, as even if it is plausible that regular role-playing shapes the character of a child, it doesn't follow from this it is a mistake ever to allow kids to observe imitators at work. That it would do them no good to pretend repeatedly they were themselves tightfisted crustaceans or uptight cephalopods or immature and clueless echinoderms or porifera doesn't by itself entail they'll be harmed irreparably or even at all by a few short episodes, or even a full-length feature film depicting the undersea misadventures of a certain

Spongebob Squarepants. Socrates returns to the theme of imitation towards the end of the book, where he does provide further arguments regarding its harmful impact not only on participants but on spectators as well. Specifically, he considers the damage it does both to the thought and the action of those affected by it. He is, at the same time, uncharacteristically cautious regarding the conclusions they draw there, and we should be cautious, too, in considering them definitive. While he starts out claiming that what had impressed him most about their entire discussion so far was their decision to ban most poets from the ideal city, he concludes by inviting poets and poetry lovers to defend their art, and to show that it can be not only pleasing but beneficial.

Socrates says of the works of tragic poets and other imitators that "all such things seem to maim the thought of those who hear them and do not as a remedy have the knowledge of how they really are" (595b). To explain, he argues that imitations are two degrees removed from true reality, and nevertheless manage to shape the opinions of the ignorant, leading them to think they understand things with which they are unacquainted. Speaking with Glaucon, he poses the following question:

"Could you tell me what imitation in general is? For I myself scarcely comprehend what it wants to be."

(595c)

In order to get started, he reminds Glaucon that when they try to make sense of anything, they start out by attempting to define the form its many instances share. There are many couches, for example, but there is something about each that makes it a couch and not a table. Whatever that is, he calls its form or idea. Because there wouldn't be any couches without the form of a couch – that is, unless there was something that it is to be a couch – each can be said to owe its existence to this form or idea; and because each couch wouldn't be a couch unless it fulfilled the expectations contained within the idea, each can be said to imitate and approximate this idea as well. Those who don't grasp what it is to be a couch can never encounter couches around them – or if they did they wouldn't know what to make of them or do with them.

When a carpenter builds a couch, he does not invent its form, but rather looks to the form as a model. He knows what it is and ought to be to be a couch, and then he makes something that fits the idea. The same is true of anything. Each thing is what it is, by exhibiting a characteristic set of attributes, unified in a specific way. The many things that make up the world, both living and dead, natural and invented, fall into categories and exhibit characteristics and patterns of activity that define them, and Socrates has Glaucon consider the question who or what it might be that invented these patterns.

Glaucon expresses doubt that there could be such a creator, and Socrates says that anyone could create anything in the simplest of ways.

> "It's not hard," I said. "You could fabricate them quickly in many ways and most quickly, of course, if you are willing to take a mirror and carry it around everywhere; quickly you will make the sun and the things in the heaven; quickly, the earth; and quickly, yourself and the other animals and implements and plants and everything else that was just now mentioned."
>
> "Yes," he said, "so that they look like they are; however, they surely are not in truth."
>
> (596d–e)

This, Socrates suggests, is the essence of imitation. It merely copies existing forms. It doesn't create them. Painters and poets, he argues, do just this kind of thing. Taking once again the example of the couch, he distinguishes between three different kinds of couches: there is the form of couch, its definition or idea; then there is the individual couch, created by a carpenter, who has this idea in mind; finally there is the copy of that couch, depicted by a painter or described by the poet. He says that while the carpenter imitates the idea, attempting to create the best couch she can by getting as clear as she can about what it is and ought to be, the painter or poet looks to this or that couch, and attempts to create an image that looks like a part of it, as it appears from one side, or puts the listener in mind of some aspect of a specific couch.

He concludes that what we can learn from imitation is extremely limited.

> "Therefore, imitation is surely far from the truth; and, as it seems, it is due to this that it produces everything – because it lays hold of a certain small part of each thing, and that part is itself only a phantom. For example, the painter, we say, will paint for us a shoemaker, a carpenter, and the other craftsmen, although he doesn't understand the arts of any of them. But, nevertheless, if he is a good painter, by painting a carpenter and displaying him from far off, he would deceive children and foolish human beings into thinking that it is truly a carpenter."
>
> (598b–c)

The distinction he draws here – between the idea of something that defines what it is to be that thing, its various instances, and images or imitations of it – should sound familiar from the allegory of the cave. There's a significant difference, though, and it is worth spelling out here. The things existing outside the cave, from which the statues are copied, correspond to the ideas or forms; the statues themselves correspond to the actual things around us, the many instances of the forms – the sun and stars, the earth and its animals, people, tables and chairs – the furniture of the world. The shadows are their variable appearances, how they seem to us, as they change and as we change our opinions about them. Here, however, he distinguishes between things and their images, rather than between things and their appearances. Appearances – the shadows – are how things seem to us, from a specific perspective and under certain assumptions. Images are deliberately constructed, imitating aspects of the things they aim to depict. Imitation, says Socrates, "lays hold of a certain small part of each thing," such as the way things appear to the painter at a certain moment or from a certain point of view, "and that part is itself only a phantom" (598b). In the case of the painted image, for instance, it is neither the thing itself nor even its appearance. It is, by contrast, a copy of the appearance, an attempt to capture its fleeting show, on the part of a skilled artist or artisan.

The difference, then, between appearances and images seems to be that one is spontaneous and natural, the other deliberate and constructed. If appearances are removed from the truth, then images would appear even further. In fact, later on, Socrates suggests that what the imitator copies is not so much things as popular opinions about them: "as it seems, whatever looks to be fair to the many who don't know anything – that he will imitate" (602b). Still, the hesitation expressed in his words seems appropriate, as in the passage that follows he places imitations also "third from the truth," just like the shadows that the prisoners witness. While the difference between images or imitations, on the one hand, and appearances on the other, appears obvious enough, perhaps this appearance is also removed from the truth. Perhaps this appearance of an obvious difference masks a deeper affinity between both. Perhaps it is to draw our attention to this affinity that Socrates in the allegory has it that the shadows are cast by statues, products of artifice made to imitate something real. That the shadowy procession is not itself natural, but staged for the prisoners as a kind of shadow puppet play, suggests that Socrates was hinting at a deeper affinity between everyday experience and imitative art than his interlocutors pick up on either in the original discussion of art or in the subsequent introduction of the allegorical cave. Perhaps it is to remedy this failure, at least in the minds of his attentive readers, that Plato has Socrates return to the topic of imitation in the final book of the *Republic*, after they had ostensibly resolved the major questions of the dialogue.

Whether Plato intended this or didn't, we should consider it. A merit of his approach to writing philosophy is that it invites reader participation, provoking questions not only about what is said but about what is suggestively omitted as well. To read a Platonic dialogue with care is to find oneself a part of its audience, listening in on Socrates' conversations, perhaps unable or unwilling to interrupt but always needing to reflect. When we do consider comparisons between the appearances of reality represented by the shadows and the imitations of reality created by painters and poets and other artisans, it calls attention to the fact that appearances themselves, the way things seem to us to be, are also constructs. What we encounter all around us is not what is there in truth, but our interpretation of things, the way they seem to us in light of our abilities to discern, our capacities to distinguish, and our interests and assumptions. The old, drunken man whom Alex and his droogs accost on the street, for example, could as easily appear to be a man in need of assistance, as an eyesore to be eliminated. A child who didn't understand homelessness or drunkenness might just be confused or see someone on the ground sick. Someone else might not even notice. While some interpretations will turn out to be correctable mistakes, as if another didn't see a man there at all but only a pile of rubbish, real differences in how things appear can also rest on varying standards and values. How this or any situation appears to anyone depends on how he has been raised, his past experiences, his ideas about the world, and his sense of what matters. These factors are not fixed by nature, but for the most part result from education and culture, from politics, from religion, or the idiosyncrasies of an upbringing.

The stories we encounter and our exposure to various media depicting the world around us are also significant factors, yet the fact we can know or learn that these aren't real, but rather imitations or representations, means we can reflect upon them as stories, reflect upon their meanings and the interests behind them, in ways we rarely do when we consider appearances obvious or inevitable. The ability to reflect upon the meanings behind the stories we tell, to ask questions about the assumptions they deliver, to grasp that there is always more to reality than the ways it is depicted, and there are always many ways to depict it – this ability, when applied to appearances, provides just the insight that initiates philosophy.

What Plato suggests by having Socrates imply a comparison between appearances and imitations or images, is that what we take to be real is itself an imitation. What we take to be real is not reality itself, in other words, but is a picture we paint or the story that we tell ourselves in order to make sense of it. What is more, by depicting appearances themselves – the shadow plays inside the cave – to be the results of deliberate artifice, Socrates suggests that the stories we tell and the pictures we paint are not exclusively our own. They are shaped by others, by fathers and mothers, educators and politicians, into something that appears inevitable, just the way things are. As a result of our educations, the assumptions and values that give shape to appearances come to seem to us nothing more than common sense.

The difference between ordinary appearance, then, and images or imitations is not that the latter are deliberate or constructed and the former natural and inevitable, but that in the case of images or imitations we are or can easily become aware of the artifice. This difference is critical. Socrates does say that a skillful imitator can fool the young and the ignorant into thinking they encounter there the very real thing. The first step in knowledge, as Socrates insists in his *Apology*, is to know what it is you do not know, which suggests that insofar as the imitation shows itself to be an imitation our encounter with it can deliver greater insight than an appearance which seems to be real. It is, perhaps, this Socratic wisdom that can serve as the remedy preventing imitations from maiming the thought of those who experience them. The encounter with imitations might also serve as a remedy to free us from the chains that bind us to appearances, insofar as by investigating imitations, how they work to communicate and reflect realities partially, we can begin to understand the workings of appearances that we, ordinarily, fail to see are also constructs. The capacity for the critical investigation of images can develop into a critical stance with respect to appearances themselves. That's not the usual aim of the imitative arts, which tend to focus more on entertaining than on educating the masses, and to achieve this end they can't risk upsetting their audiences by throwing their assumptions in their faces.

Still, for its capacity to call attention to the artificiality of the assumptions informing ordinary experience, we might expect the art of imitation to stand in close relation to philosophy. A skillful imitator should not only be able to confuse the ignorant but also to educate and illuminate by focusing the attention of her audiences on those aspects of their situation they might have overlooked in the grip of their assumptions. For those who aren't fooled by the imitation, comparisons between the way things seem to them and the way things are presented in the imitation can also be instructive, provoking questions that unsettle their assumptions, loosening chains that hold them fast in the cave. In fact, Socrates himself on a number of occasions suggests a need to employ images, such as the allegory of the cave itself, which imitate certain aspects of the human condition in order to illuminate where we tend to be confused. Insofar as imitators call attention to or remind us of the limits of opinions drawn from appearances, their works could function as philosophical provocations. Socrates casts doubt on precisely this, however, suggesting that more often than signaling the limits of our opinions poetic imitations tend to confirm us in them. Even the greatest poets and painters depict realities they seem to understand, and their works seem to deliver insights into those realities, when in fact they possess only superficial knowledge of what they depict, and in reality teach very little.

Socrates continues his investigation of imitation by considering whether tragic poets have real insights into the things they speak of in their works. If so, they would appear actually to possess the wisdom that to which philosophy aspires.

> "Then, next," I said, "tragedy and its leader, Homer, must be considered, since we hear from some that these men know all arts and all things human that have to do with virtue and vice, and the divine things too. For it is necessary that the good poet, if he is going to make fair poems about the things his poetry concerns, be in possession of knowledge when he makes his poems or not be able to make them. Hence, we must consider whether those who tell us this have encountered these imitators and been deceived; and whether, therefore, seeing their works, they do not recognize that these works are third from what is and are easy to make for the man who doesn't know the truth – for such a man makes what look like beings but are not. Or, again, is there also something to what they say, and do the good poets really know about the things that, in the opinion of the many, they say well?"
>
> (598e–599a)

Socrates and his interlocutors decide that if someone were able both to make something and make a copy or imitation of it, he would consider it more honorable to make the thing itself. Likewise it would be better to do great deeds than depict them in a poem, to heal people rather than describe the work of doctors, and to lead rather than give an account of the governance of others. Homer, they agree, did nothing of the sort. It is clear, then, that he doesn't understand the arts he describes, but only how to imitate their appearances.

> "Then, in this way, I suppose we'll claim the poetic man also uses names and phrases to color each of the arts. He himself doesn't

understand; but he imitates in such a way as to seem, to men whose condition is like his own and who observe only speeches, to speak very well. He seems to do so when he speaks using meter, rhythm, and harmony, no matter whether the subject is shoemaking, generalship, or anything else. So great is the charm that these things by nature possess. For when the things of the poets are stripped of the colors of the music and are said alone, by themselves, I suppose you know how they look. For you, surely, have seen."

"I have indeed," he said.

"Don't they," I said, "resemble the faces of boys who are youthful but not fair in what happens to their looks when the bloom has forsaken them?"

"Exactly," he said.

"Come now, reflect on this. The maker of the phantom, the imitator, we say, understands nothing of what is but rather of what looks like it is. Isn't that so?"

"Yes."

(601a–c)

Regarding Homer and the other great tragedians, Socrates poses a dilemma: either they understand the subjects they cover in their works or they merely imitate their appearance, saying of them only what seems likely to fool the ignorant. If, for example, Homer depicts a doctor providing medical advice, Socrates asks whether it's likely to be sound or whether it's more likely to sound like what people think a doctor is likely to say. If Homer and Hesiod really were able to accomplish great things or educate people and make them truly better, Socrates argues, their compatriots would have compelled them to do this rather than spend their time travelling and reciting their poems. If Homer's ability to portray leaders, such as politicians and generals, reflected a true understanding of politics and the art of war, Socrates argues, we should expect he would have led, he would have actually founded cities, or maybe gone to battle. That he did no such thing, that he led no armies or cities, and that, further, he invented nothing and educated no one, suggests that he was not himself wise in any of these ways, but merely possessed the skill to speak about such things convincingly to those, like him, who lacked knowledge. Of course great film directors, such as Kubrick, might as well be generals. Despite his famous failure to bring to screen the definitive Napoleon epic that he worked on for years, Stanley Kubrick certainly went to metaphorical war, commanding troops and winning battles, and accomplished astonishing works of art as a result.

Art's potential

No one among his interlocutors notes it, but we should consider that this suggestion – if they truly had knowledge they ought to be leaders and educators rather than writers and rhapsodes – resembles closely a proposal developed earlier in connection with the allegory of the cave. There Socrates argues that the true philosopher, who escapes from the cave and learns to contemplate the way things really are rather than how they seem to the masses, should be compelled to return to the cave, to educate and lead. In the case of philosophers, it is their inability or unwillingness to put their thinking into practice that makes the multitudes misunderstand them or consider their insights ridiculous. When it comes to the poet, the same incapacity suggests to the philosopher that his accomplishments are frivolous. This conclusion depends upon an assumption that it is better to accomplish great deeds than describe them. As evidence, Socrates cites the fact that the greatest honors accrue to those who act. What is apparently not considered is whether composing great works is itself a great deed, deserving of the kind of praise that was in fact bestowed upon the greatest of Greek poets, and upon great writers, artists, actors, and filmmakers in our own age. At the same time it suggests the possibility that this praise is misplaced, that we praise poets and imitators for the wrong kinds of things, for being popular rather than providing real benefit to their audiences, for educating and improving them.

In order to motivate the conclusion that painters and poets are lacking in knowledge, Socrates focuses specifically on their depictions of skilled individuals: shoemakers, carpenters, doctors, and other experts. To show they don't know the subjects they depict, he asks whether one who paints, say, a portrait of a shoemaker, knows what it takes to make a shoe, or whether someone, like Homer, who portrays a leader's acts himself knows how to lead. There's something odd about that way of posing the question whether imitators know their subject matter, because of course we don't expect a general to recite poetry or a cobbler to paint. What we should ask, instead, is whether imitators have distinctive insights of their own, whether there's a wisdom involved in depiction that's distinct from the wisdom involved in the subject depicted. Certainly, skill is required for imitation, for depicting things so that they resemble closely the original. "If he is a good painter," Socrates notes, "by painting a carpenter and displaying him from far off, he would deceive children and foolish human beings into thinking that it is truly a carpenter" (598c). What is at stake here, however, is not whether the imitator can only fool the foolish but whether she can teach the teachable, whether the imitator has insights of her own, communicated in her works.

This criticism of the imitator bears a striking resemblance to one brought against filmmakers when, in the early years of cinema, certain critics objected to the notion that film could be an art form at all. They held that what filmmakers did was merely record reality mechanically, by way of a machine, and that as "artists" they added nothing to it. Even if the recording was of something dramatized and staged deliberately, the true art then should be considered that of theater, and since the camera merely copied the staged production, the so-called "art" of the filmmaker was derivative. Rudolph Arnheim, an influential art critic and one of the first such to consider film to be a distinctive art form, answered the objections powerfully.

First of all, he pointed out, film does not merely reproduce reality. As a representative medium, it has a number of built-in limitations. The cinematic image is two-dimensional and flat, and there is no intrinsic sense of scale or dimension to its image, given that a landscape or a face can fill the same-sized screen. Even time itself can be prolonged or sped up, and distances elided through editing. In its early years, at least, film reduced the complexity of reality to its visual aspects, and even there eliminated color. Moreover, especially in the early days of film, decent exposure of the image required massive and powerful lighting, and how the light was arranged made (and still makes) an enormous difference to the final product. Given these restrictions, the filmmaker must be selective in capturing just those aspects of the natural or staged reality she's interested in, and decide how to present it from the most favorable perspective. It is precisely the limitations of the medium, he argued, that demand creativity on the part of the filmmaker, and require that she possess a "feeling for the objects" she's depicting, allowing her to determine how to deliver their best or most characteristic view. He offers the example of a cube, which could be shot straight on, showing only a square, or from an elevated position centered on an upper corner, revealing it far more fully as an object with multiple sides, three visible and three hidden. In fact the reduction of depth combined with the moving transformations of the frame's perspective – this "welcome element of unreality" (Arnheim, *Film as Art*, p. 60) – allows the filmmaker to deliberately hide and reveal selectively elements of the reality she records. A camera movement might surprise us, showing that what we took to be a square turned out to be a cube. The richest cinematic images, he argues, are those that exploit the limitations of cinema in order to reveal reality all the more richly.

Socrates says of the imitator that what he imitates is not the way things are but how they appear, and he illustrates the difference with the example of the couch, which is the same couch whether you observe it from the side or the front or from any other perspective. In spite of the fact that these perspectives upon it appear all different, in truth it is one thing that does not differ from itself at all. In presenting its aspects separately, the imitator is not looking to what it really is but only to how it looks. "Therefore," he insists, "imitation is surely far from the truth; and, as it seems, it is due to this that it produces everything – because it lays hold of a certain small part of each thing, and that part is merely a phantom" (598b), not the real thing at all but only its seeming or appearance, only a part masquerading as the whole. In that respect it is no different from ordinary experience, in which we can only encounter aspects of the things around us, one side or salient feature at a time. We never see the full cube, for example, and much less the full person, even those we say we know and care about. We experience things piecemeal, only this or that aspect or element in a given moment.

Yet to know things is to know precisely *that* about them: that we don't know them entirely in the aspects they reveal to us. The cube has many sides, which we can't see all at once. To know the cube is to know this. A person has more aspects than we can ever see at all, because we cannot know what facets of their character or capacities will emerge in response to new and unpredictable situations. At the same time, as Arnheim notes, a thoughtful artist, whether painter or photographer or filmmaker, can select those perspectives that reveal an object more and less fully, that don't show everything directly but show clearly what is hidden. Likewise, a storyteller or poet can often select for depiction those aspects of a person that manage to encapsulate the richest and most characteristic features of his or her identity, and at the same time make clear where mysteries yet remain. What Socrates appears to overlook – but Plato likely means to suggest to the attentive reader of his remarks – is that "the one" truth of things, that binds their complex manifold aspects or appearances, can be intimated powerfully through a creatively and thoughtfully selected presentation of "a certain small part of each thing" – merely shadow or perspective.

Socrates' selection of skilled artisans as his primary examples of what painters and poets might portray does make clear, and the ensuing discussion draws this out, that their ability to depict specific subjects convincingly does not entail they know all there is to know about those subjects, or even anything of what those subjects know. At the same time, it begs the question whether the poetic imitator has any special skill, over and above the ability to speak "using meter, rhythm and harmony, whether the subject is shoemaking, generalship or anything else" (601a–b). It begs the question whether, perhaps, there might be something that the poet or painter might know about the artisan that she does not know about herself. It is this kind of knowledge, self-knowledge, that in his *Apology* Socrates argues skilled artisans don't possess. Knowing something well – how to craft this or that product – they take themselves to be wise in other respects. Of course, Socrates says the same there of politicians and poets as well: poets, in particular, say many fine things about which they have no special insights; when it comes to making sense of what they say, their listeners are at least as competent as they are. If poetry involves any kind of skill, it is a different kind of skill than that of other artisans. Indeed it seems not to be a skill at all, but a matter of what Socrates suggests is divine inspiration, and what in more modern times has been called "genius."

To be a skilled artisan is to be able to produce reliably an outcome or product that serves a specific purpose. Socrates considers the difference between the craftsman and the imitator in ways that highlight precisely this fact. Considering objects created by artisans, he distinguishes between the one who uses them, the one who makes them, and the one who imitates them. A rider, for example, makes use of the horse's bridle; a leatherworker makes it; a painter paints it; and a poet describes it. It is the rider, he says, who has genuine knowledge of a bridle, both what it is and what it ought to be, for the rider knows its uses and knows what it needs to be like to serve those uses well. The leatherworker follows directions of the rider, making the bridle to the rider's specifications, and his skill consists of an ability to meet the rider's needs reliably. The imitator, by contrast, needn't know what it does or how it does it, but merely what it looks like or how it appears to those who don't know. As Socrates notes, the poet "himself doesn't understand; but he imitates in such a way as to seem, to men whose condition is like his own and who observe only speeches, to speak very well" (601a). The distinction is somewhat questionable, especially in the case of a poet like Homer who sometimes describes quite precisely what his heroes do with their implements. In some cases, at least, the experts could agree that how the imitator depicts their subjects was perceptive. More importantly, though, what poets often do quite well, that goes beyond an insight into what things are and need to be, is to illuminate the purposes served in using them well. When Homer describes his hero's sword, it matters little whether he could make one himself or wield it with skill, but matters a great deal whether he helps us understand why the hero employed it in just the ways he did and what the outcome of his actions meant for all who were affected. Skilled warriors are not always wise, and a thoughtful poet can make their foolish aims clear. To take a later example, the tragic poet Sophocles may lack both the skill in battle and the wisdom in ruling possessed by Oedipus, and yet the aim of his tragedies is precisely to reveal that even the great and powerful cannot know what they do not know and that it will lead to their downfall.

If we apply the distinction between users and makers, further, to poetic imitations themselves, we can ask what is the use for which they are purposefully created. To answer that, we'd need to consider who is the proper user, who can specify their proper use. It makes a great deal of difference, and much of Socrates' discussion is directed to showing what a difference it makes, if we consider the user of such creations to be the many who enjoy them, or the few who employ them. From the standpoint of the typical audience, what makes a poetic work worthwhile is that it gives pleasure or amusement. They like to be entertained, they'd rather not be bored. Socrates admits that the works of a number of imitators certainly accomplish this aim. From the standpoint of the politician, by contrast, the merit of poetic works is that they impact their audiences in ways that serve the interests of the city. It is the overall aim of the *Republic*, moreover, to show that the interests of the city and of its citizens coincide – that the city is best and its citizens happiest when they live well and are just. It follows, then, that from a political standpoint the aim of poetic art should be to educate and improve the character of its citizens.

This aim, however, is not one that skill alone can accomplish. Early in *The Apology*, Socrates reports speaking to a man about raising his sons. "If your sons were colts or calves," he asked,

> "we could find and engage a supervisor for them who would make them excel in their proper qualities, some horse breeder or farmer. Now since they are men, whom do you have in mind to supervise them? Who is an expert in this kind of excellence, the human and social kind? I think you must have given thought to this since you have sons. Is there such a person … or is there not?"
>
> (20a–b)

There is someone, the man responds, a self-proclaimed wise man, or "sophist," who promises to improve young men, whom he'd already hired at the low price of five minae. The idea that moral education is akin to training horses might seem outrageous; compare, however, the popularity of therapists and self-help gurus who promise to fix kids or marriages or lifestyles over the course of a weekend retreat. We might also consider the scientists from *A Clockwork Orange*, who promised the Minister they could supply a technical solution to the problem of immorality and criminality.

Socrates calls such claims into question throughout Plato's many works, by demonstrating that education requires serious and sustained initiative on the part of the educated, and pointing out that even great men with a reputation for wisdom and virtue had often failed to raise children like themselves. His reminder that Homer himself had no reputation for improving his own loved ones suggests the same is true of poets. Whatever wisdom or skill they may possess, it is not such as to achieve its aims reliably, even where those aims are clear to the poet, who can understandably be ambivalent about the relative importance of creating works that appeal to the many and creating works that deliver truths.

Education, Socrates suggests, is not at all like horse training or any other craft; it is not a skill that invariably or usually produces the intended result. This is so, whether the educator is poet, sophist, or philosopher. The educator can at best establish conditions for learning, but there are no guarantees. Real learning is internal, and not a matter of imposing or delivering knowledge from without. It requires a willingness on the part of the student to take it seriously. The educator, we can say, merely poses the questions, and the student needs to make an effort to propose the answers. Then she needs to be willing and able to revise her convictions and actions in light of what a consideration of the implications of her answers demonstrates.

Socrates often spoke to those who didn't take seriously the concerns he raised for them. Or, they attempted repeatedly to turn conversations in directions that would support their self-conceptions. In the dialogue named after him, for example, Meno asks Socrates whether virtue can be taught. Upon investigation, it is clear that what he means by virtue is whatever qualities the wealthy and powerful possess that give them their wealth and honor and power. What he wants is for someone to tell him what he can do to gain such things, without essentially changing who he is. For a person like him, virtue can only appear as a matter of luck or a gift from the gods. He continually pushes back at Socrates' efforts to lead him to see that without making an effort, without being willing to put his character, reputation, and opinions on the line, he will never accomplish real and meaningful change. Real improvement requires not only a competent teacher but a willing pupil, one who does not resist the insights made possible through their interactions.

The same is, clearly, true of whatever pedagogical merit stories may possess. It is not simply a matter of the story or storyteller, but of their audience's way of taking up what they offer. Interpretations and emphasis can differ widely based on the predispositions of a story's audience. We see this clearly in the story of Alex, for example, who impresses the prison Chaplain by taking a strong liking to the Bible. What we see is that he only liked the gory and sexy bits, identifying himself with their perpetrators rather than sympathizing with their victims. We see him seated in the prison library, a large Bible before him, rapt in attention, mouthing words with apparent piety, a beatific look upon his face. The frame shifts then to his visions, an image of Christ bearing his cross and being whipped from behind by an unseen man yelling "Move along there!" We might guess he identifies with Christ's sufferings, that his stint in prison has made him feel remorse. Then the camera pans to show Alex himself wielding the whip, dressed in the gear of a Roman centurion, and we hear him narrate in an eager voice, "and I could viddy myself helping out and even taking charge of the tolchoking and the nailing in, being dressed in the height of Roman fashion." He imagines fighting alongside the Israelites, drinking "Hebrew vino," and then making love with concubines. He complains, to us, about the boring and preachy bits in the latter part of the Bible. Stories, clearly, can be taken up selectively, and no storyteller can guarantee that an audience will respond as expected.

Much of the remaining discussion of imitative artists in the *Republic* focuses on the question whether they do or don't improve their audiences. No longer exclusively interested in the kinds of poetry, storytelling, and music that educate young guardians, Socrates explores the impact of the imitative arts on anyone exposed to them. The concerns he raises, building upon those explored in his earlier remarks on education, are significant and shouldn't easily be dismissed. At the same time, they don't so much demonstrate the worthlessness of the entire enterprise, as identify intrinsic challenges that might conceivably be addressed. They identify the problems, in other words, that a serious defense of the worth of poetic imitation will need to show itself capable of overcoming, if not in every instance at least in some. A brief summary of these difficulties, gathered together with those touched upon already, will prepare the way to follow up on certain hints Socrates leaves as to how imitation, in at least some of its incarnations, might manage to redeem itself.

Socrates' worries, as mentioned already, have to do with whose interests are served by the imitative arts. That their works are appealing is not the issue; Socrates notes in his previous discussion that the imitative poet is "by far the most pleasing to boys and their teachers, and to the great mob too" (397d). He suggests that such an artist deserves great praise, but should nevertheless be sent away to another city whose citizens are less concerned by the educational impact of the arts. He does offer an explanation for why such works are pleasing. It is that they appeal to something lower in our natures than our capacity for reasoning. Human beings are able to reflect upon their course of action, to resist what appeals to them naturally. Our desires, though, must be kept in check, resisted where they would lead us to behave inappropriately. The tension within the soul, between its inclinations and its decisions, is something that can't be portrayed effectively by art – precisely because it is a tension within the soul. In order to portray someone who overcomes desires, stories, songs, and portraits need first to portray that person overcome by desire: lusting, yielding to anger and self-pity, and laughing at the misfortunes of others. Only then can they effectively portray that character resisting such urges. Portrayals of those who resist desires without first yielding to them lack drama, lack excitement. They appear to be indifferent and uncaring, rather than characters who deliberately overcome desires. Portrayals of them yielding first excite audiences by appealing to their pride, their lust, their self-pity.

Regarding the way that tragic poetry appeals to self-pity, Socrates says:

> If you are aware that what is then held down by force in our own misfortunes and has hungered for tears and sufficient lament and satisfaction, since it is by nature such as to desire these things, is that which now gets satisfaction and enjoyment from the poets. What is by nature best in us, because it hasn't been adequately educated by argument or habit, relaxes its guard over this mournful part because it sees another's sufferings, and it isn't shameful for it, if some other man who claims to be good laments out of season, to praise and pity him; rather it believes that it gains the pleasure and wouldn't permit itself to be deprived of it by despising the whole poem. I suppose that only a certain few men are capable of calculating that the enjoyment of other people's sufferings has a necessary effect on one's own. For the pitying part, fed strong on these examples, is not easily held down in one's own suffering.
>
> (606a–b)

Such portrayals deliver vicarious thrills, and we do not resist them as we might in real life because we associate the feelings with a character from a story. What we fail to perceive, however, is that satisfying such urges vicariously has an impact on our own character. We develop habits of self-pity, or of yielding to lust or anger, that we'd otherwise consider inappropriate. The argument bears a striking similarity with certain Freudian accounts of the arts that claim they appeal to unconscious urges we would otherwise repress. Notably *A Clockwork Orange* has been considered in that light, where Alex's irrepressible violence has been held to satisfy anti-social tendencies existing latent in most of us. The difference is that Freudian accounts hold the vicarious satisfaction of such urges to be healthy, since unsatisfied urges return in unpredictable ways. By contrast, Socrates suggests that their gratification harms us, by cultivating habits for reading situations in light of our desires. Regular consumption of heterosexual, male-oriented pornography, for example, has often been considered to make its viewers more likely to interpret women as sex objects. In that case, the image creates an ideal, of catering to male desire, in terms of which male consumers learn to assess the women they encounter in everyday life.

Certainly, that seems to be true of Alex. While the effect of the so-called "Ludovico Technique" is to condition him to feel disgust where he'd previously felt lust, it's unlikely he came by his original desires naturally or spontaneously. He appears, rather, to have already been conditioned by the images and examples he finds all around him. Erotic and pornographic images abound in his world, and the impact upon him and his peers seems to be that they can't see a younger woman without considering her a candidate for what he calls, crudely, "the old in-out in-out," and this is so whether she claims to want it or not. Women, as he considers them, appear only as mother figures to be manipulated and appeased or as erotic objects, inviting his desires to subdue and master sexually.

Consider, for example, the nature of the images that appear on the walls of nearly every interior, such as those in the house of the woman he murdered, who stayed there alone with her numerous cats. Apart from a large, phallic statue – which becomes the unexpected murder weapon – that she asks him not to touch because it is "an important work of art," the paintings on the wall are all of women, provocatively posed to reveal a highly sexual and aroused body, but, even more prominently, looking straight at the viewer with faces that encourage a leering eye. The look on these faces, as with much pornographic imagery, appears to welcome the lustful eye. They are faces the individuality of which is effaced. To see a face, as we noticed previously, is not merely to see an object but is to see what sees, and to see oneself seen. What these faces seem to see and solicit is arousal on the part of their viewer. It is a look of desire, which desires precisely to be taken as an object of desire. They invite their viewer to see them not as a face, in other words, but a body to be desired. It is not, therefore, a look that challenges the objectifying gaze of its viewer, but rather invites its viewer to gaze with lust. It is no wonder that, surrounded by such images, Alex and his droogs would develop the habit of seeing women generally in this light.

Plato's primary concern regarding imitative artworks, then, is that they lead us to feel things we should not and, in particular, to feel sympathy with courses of action that are inconsistent with how a "good person," or one whose decisions followed her assessments of what is best, would behave. Imitative arts provoke us to feel self-pity, lust, and anger, and thereby condition us to imitate the self-pitying, lustful, and violent person. They condition us to follow immediate inclinations, and to place such feelings above the standards we endorse upon reflection. They condition us, put another way, to interpret situations we find ourselves in as calling for sexual activity, violence, and tears.

Imitative arts call attention, at the same time, to our capacity to be of many minds about the very same subject matter, to respond to it ambiguously. We can be excited and aroused, for example, by activities that would horrify us in everyday life. This can happen, though, precisely because we are aware of a difference between the imitation and everyday life. We weep for the weeping character, when we wouldn't weep for ourselves. We are enraged by the antagonist, and cheer on the hero in the violence he wields upon him. We are aroused by acts of sexuality on screen that we wouldn't permit in ourselves, precisely because we think they won't affect us. To take an example from cinema, we do not worry about the collateral damage inflicted upon innocent bystanders as James Bond accomplishes his missions, we root for him, even if we'd be terrified were we to find ourselves in the crowded streets he recklessly plows through in a fancy car in pursuit of his target.

The distance between imitative fiction and reality both allows it to appeal to emotions we'd otherwise find troubling, and entails that we can and do distinguish between these fictions and everyday life. It is our capacity for thought that makes the distinction; our capacity to feel links us to the action. Something we noted in the discussion of Alex's treatment is that it is not enough to know what is right; we need to feel it as well. The imitative arts, as illustrated powerfully by Kubrick's *A Clockwork Orange*, have the power to link and de-link our cognitive and affective responses to a situation – they can make us think one way and feel another, or can communicate feelings in ways that go far beyond mere argument. Perhaps, as suggested already, this insight into the unreality of imitations is precisely the remedy that prevents them from maiming the thought of those who hear or encounter them. That they present to us situations very like life, evoking thoughts and feelings associated with what is real, may offer an advantage for reflection that we don't have in relation to situations we are closer to or embedded in.

We can reflect upon the feelings and thoughts evoked by such works, and consider whether they're legitimate or appropriately developed.

The interlocutors of Socrates are often too close to the subject matters they discuss – they feel themselves under scrutiny, they feel themselves judged, and they resist. At the same time, much of philosophy can feel abstract, disconnected from the concerns of everyday life. Reflections upon the meanings and values embedded in narrative imitations provide an opportunity to combine the distance necessary for reflection with the closeness required to care. There is always the danger that they get too close. They may, as Socrates notes, manage to fool fools and children, and perhaps Stanley Kubrick was right to endorse a ban on *A Clockwork Orange* in Britain, where there was a real risk it would inspire copycats. That doesn't mean, though, that it has nothing to teach those prepared to take it seriously, reflecting on its workings and the questions it poses. That doesn't mean reflections upon such works are useless to those who possess the remedy of insight into their unreality, and then learn to apply that insight more broadly. Imitative artworks such as films have the capacity to remind us that even our experience of everyday life is a construction, a product of attitudes and values that we rarely acknowledge or reflect on. To draw upon the imagery of the allegory of the cave, imitative artworks are not so much copies of shadows as part of the shadows themselves, part of the domain of everyday life and experience. Yet we possess a distinct advantage in relation to these shadows, that are manifestly not real, and reflection upon the ways that they nevertheless win our convictions and concerns can teach us a great deal about the assumptions and values we employ in making sense of the rest.

Our relation to imitative artworks, and in particular the works of cinema, is not obviously worse than our relation to appearances or the experience of everyday life. We stand, in relation to these works, in some ways better and some ways worse than Plato's prisoners stand in relation to the shadows. We are worse, because they affect us early on when we're unwitting and the worst of them can work to solidify the prejudices and habits that prevent us from thinking and operating otherwise than in accordance with our inclinations and common sense. We are better off, because we can distinguish these images from everyday life. In their imitation of appearance, films have the potential to push audiences to reflect upon the nature of appearance, and on the distinction between what is real and what is apparent. In their imitation of action, films provoke ethical questions, regarding what actions are appropriate or acceptable. They require interpretation and provoke critical assessments, and can lead us to reflect upon appropriate standards for interpretation and aesthetic assessment. Questions about reality and appearance, ethics, art, interpretation, and evidence – questions tied to the core traditional themes of philosophy – arise naturally in relation to cinema, and some films pose such questions deliberately.

Consider Kubrick's film and its way of posing philosophical questions. *A Clockwork Orange* directly poses the question of the existence of freedom and the question what it means to be free, by presenting the Ludovico treatment as something that takes away freedom. Just as the film does not simply endorse Alex's anti-social infatuation with aesthetic ultraviolence, it does not, either, insist it is always wrong for the state to supplant or impose upon free will, since it never even clearly suggests that Alex was free. It suggests, rather, that the so-called free-dom enjoyed by Alex even prior to his treatment is in fact an illusion. The conception of freedom we require in order to make sense of the film's depiction of Alex is not the "all or nothing" notion of individual freedom that seems so obvious to modern sensibilities. It is, rather, a more complex notion of a capacity for choice emerging from competing drives within, and fostered from without, a notion that is in fact remarkably close to the character of justice that Socrates outlines in the *Republic*. The film also, in its depiction of Alex as storyteller, and specifically as a storyteller whose account of his reality is partial and problematic, poses the question of the relation between reality as such and the perspectives and construals through which alone we can access it.

The film poses ethical questions, both by way of its influence on its viewers and for its depiction of its central character, Alex. The film's presentation of Alex, and of his circumstances, is not simply neutral, but amounts to an assessment of both his character and activities, and of the justice of the actions of the state, assessments that can and ought to be questioned by the viewer. The film does depict Alex as telling his own story and soliciting the viewer to feel sympathetic to his plight, but it also, as we've seen, confronts the viewer with challenges to the perspec-tive he endorses. The film thus offers a corrective to his narrative, and the sympathies it fosters. At the least the film challenges its viewers to adopt a critical perspective upon that story and its moral implications. The question of the film's actual influence on impressionable viewers, a question that overlaps directly with concerns Plato develops in the *Republic*, is one for historians and sociologists to answer, and thus beyond the scope of the present exploration. We might consider, how-ever, that the film is most likely to have a negative influence on those audiences who ignore its critical dimension. As we've seen, art can easily mislead the young and uncritical; the proper response is not to eliminate or censor the imitative arts, but to encourage audiences to be thoughtful in their responses to artworks, and to foster the creation of works that encourage the cultivation of critical responsiveness.

Bringing insights drawn from *A Clockwork Orange* into conversation (briefly) with those from the *Republic* shows that the film's response to questions of reality and freedom, justice, morality, and art is not as simplistic or unambiguous as many have considered.

5 Justice and freedom
Alex's cure

While Plato's *Republic* explores the nature of justice, *A Clockwork Orange* focuses on the importance of free will. This contrast in emphasis highlights a pivotal difference between the ancient and modern world. For the ancients, communal demands provided context and justification for the actions of the individual. Plato's *Republic* never mentions freedom, and among the Greeks, at least, the notion had much more to do with the autonomy of a people than the rights of individuals to pursue happiness as they saw fit. Still, the dialogue's account of justice as a kind of harmony in the individual soul, in which desires and passions are ruled by thought, carries with it a great deal of insight into the character of a genuine freedom. Moderns, by contrast with the ancient Greeks, consider communities just only to the extent they preserve and protect the rights of individuals. Kubrick's film complicates the point by making Alex a criminal, who clearly earned his stay in prison. It makes us wonder, however, whether he deserves to be released into society, from whose vengeance he can't defend himself. In its closing images the film hints that freedom means far more than merely the unfettered ability to act according to one's inclinations.

Justice and the nature of freedom

Following treatment, Alex is released from prison, only to discover he is no longer welcome at home. His boa constrictor is dead, a lodger has taken his room, and his parents, clearly, don't want him to stay. Things, however, go from bad to worse, in a series of misadventures that parallels almost exactly the events leading up to his arrest. He gives some change to a beggar, only to discover it is the same old man he'd beaten up in the streets. Recognizing him, the man calls upon a crowd of elderly vagrants to trample and beat him with their canes and handbags, with Alex helpless to defend himself as a result of the treatment. Luckily a couple of police turn up, but unluckily they turn out to be the very same "droogs" who'd turned on him and turned him in when they'd gotten tired of Alex calling all the shots. All grown up now and proud to have "a job for two who are now of job age," George and Dim drive him out of the city, beat him silly with their billy clubs, and nearly drown him in a cow trough. Bloodied, bruised, and tired, stumbling sadly through the dark and rain, he happens upon a home, which turns out to be that of the writer, now crippled and cared for by a muscular bodyguard. He takes Alex in, aware only of his recent infamy as the experimental subject of the government's new approach to crime. He doesn't recognize his former assailant, as the last time they'd met Alex was wearing a mask. He discovers, soon enough, when Alex gives himself away by singing in the bathtub loudly what he'd sung the time before. Now the writer, who'd planned to exploit him for political gain against the government, decides instead to get his revenge by locking him in an attic room and blasting "lovely Ludwig Van." Feeling sickness near to death, Alex decides to kill himself by leaping through the window, but only manages to land himself in a hospital with broken bones and a full body cast.

He'd eased his way through prison, by outwardly obeying rules and ingratiating himself with its chaplain, pretending to be pious. (There's only a hint in the film of the routine beatings from guards, attempted rapes from fellow inmates, and the acts of violence he suffers and perpetrates throughout his sentence, as described in the book.) It is afterwards he's truly punished, with direct retribution for his crimes from their victims, one by one, ending in a self-inflicted attempt at least at capital punishment, when Alex leaps from a window as elevated as the one he'd entered when he murdered a woman in front of her cats. The question of what is punishment and how far it is appropriate comes up directly in *A Clockwork Orange*, and is explored as well in the *Republic*, given that a familiar answer to the dialogue's central question "what is justice" is that it involves meting out punishment for crimes and rewards for good deeds.

A cosmological notion of justice and punishment comes up first, in the prison chapel. The Chaplain, gripping the podium, his face red with a righteous anger, introduces his highly skeptical and unwilling audience to the theme of divine justice and punishment. Alex, now the altar boy, is seated beside him, and a large man in the front pew leers at him, kissing and winking, as the Chaplain speaks of punishments, meted out in the flames of hell, "hotter than any earthly fire, where souls of unrepentant sinners, like yourselves..." He's interrupted when a prisoner belches loudly, the rest burst into laughter, and the Chaplain cries, "Don't you laugh! – yes, you'll burn, a fireball spinning in your screaming guts – I know, yes I know." It is, perhaps, this cosmology, of the righteous saved and sinners burning, that undergirds the Chaplain's concerns about the Ludovico treatment, for the rightness of all of this presumes that saints were freely good and sinners could have done otherwise. To cast into Hell one who was helpless could only be the act of a cruel God, unworthy of worship. Alex asks him about "this new thing they're all talking about, Father, this new treatment that gets you out of prison in no time at all," and, in order to be sure the Chaplain doesn't think that's the only reason he's interested, he tells him he just wants to be good: "I want for the rest of my life to be one act of goodness." The Chaplain objects, "goodness comes from within, goodness is... chosen. When a man cannot choose, he ceases to be a man." He repeats similar objections following the Minister of the Interior's demonstration of Alex's "cure":

> The boy has no real choice, has he? Self-interest. The fear of physi-cal pain led him to that grotesque act of self-abasement ... He ceases to be a wrongdoer. He ceases also to be a creature capable of moral choice.

Without choice, there can be no just punishment, just as there can be no merit for good deeds.

Some viewers have seized upon the Chaplain's last line as delivering the ultimate moral of the entire story, that freedom is an intrinsic good, and it would be wrong for anyone – whether God or the state – to take it away. One might need to constrain the criminal, but to compel his goodness by means of techniques is to create a moral robot, a contra-diction in terms if moral beings require choice. In short, it is to create a "Clockwork Orange." That would put the film in line with the classic response to the "problem of evil," which asks why an all-powerful and benevolent God would allow some to harm others unjustly. With the power, God could stop it. Being kind, God should want to. The classic response is that God could stop evil and disapproves, but it is a con-sequence of human freedom that some will abuse it, and without free-dom there could be no real good. Take away their freedom, and people become puppets or perfect slaves, and whatever they do is neither good nor evil but the acting out exactly of parts they never chose and can't refuse. If ridding the world of evil makes it into a puppet show devoid of moral significance, maybe it is better to allow evil now, and punish it later. We might consider this a kind of cosmic variation on the way Alex's society permits kids to roam wild and free, until they go too far, someone dies, and the kids get caught; the law then, promptly, locks them up and punishes them.

That was, at least, the "old way" of things before the new regime, and the prison governor appears to have approved. Neither he nor the Chaplain object to punishment for wrongs, but both object to the idea that you can make someone right. The governor likes the old "eye for an eye, someone hits you, you hit them back" philosophy, and thinks the state is well within its rights to punish the criminal. To deprive it of this right, by somehow fixing the wrongdoer, this "new view" of crime and punishment, he tells Alex, "seems to me to be grossly unjust, eh?"

The Minister disagrees, and shrugs off the objections of the Chaplain and the old regime as "subtleties." "We're not concerned with the motives, the higher ethics. We're concerned only with cutting down crime." Alex, notably, goes along with this. He'd worn a troubled look while the Chaplain spoke, and then looked up with pride, smiling as the Minister defended the use of the treatment. He'd already told the Chaplain when he asked about it before, and the Chaplain had first voiced his concerns, that he wasn't concerned about the "whys and wherefores." He's not interested in philosophy, in other words, he just wants what he wants: to get out. As the Minister tells the Chaplain: "the point is that it works." He and Alex agree on this point, that the outcome is what matters. For the Minister, it is curbing crime; for Alex it is being free. Everything else, they think, is just semantics.

Just what is it to be free? It's more than just another word (for nothing left to lose?). It is more than just semantics, in other words, as what matters is not so much picking definitions as getting clear about the concept, what we ought to mean when we talk about freedom. Alex is clearly wrong to think he'll be free when he gets out of prison early as a result of volunteering for the Ludovico program. He's just swapping the external constraints of the prison for a new set of internal constraints; the overpowering nausea he feels when he considers acting as he'd used to operates as a kind of conscience that can't be denied. Should we say, then, that freedom means the capacity to follow one's inclinations without any constraints?

There do seem always to be at least some constraints, operating at a more basic level than both what is socially determined and external (in this case, the prison and the institutions of government that maintain it), and what is psychological or internal (Alex's thoughts and feelings when he contemplates violence). One might hold, on account of this, that no one ever is, strictly speaking, free. If natural bodies are subject to natural laws, and our bodies are natural, then our actions, which always involve movements of the body, are also subject to natural laws. Actions are, then, determined by law – laws operative in nature and discovered by, for example, physics, chemistry, and neurophysiology. The idea that whatever happens is determined by laws is known as determinism, and some argue it is incompatible with freedom.

Noting a basic feature of natural laws, essential both to their discovery and formulation, can help to avoid this conclusion. It is that natural laws are, by their very nature, abstract. Laws of classical Newtonian physics, for example, ignore everything but mass and movement. Insofar as, in addition to its mass and movement, a thing has other structural or material properties that affect its behavior, these laws have nothing to say about that. So, for example, the law of gravity says that every massive body is attracted to every other massive body, with a force proportional to the product of their masses. Whether, however, it falls, or whether it flies, or whether it walks and talks or dances across the surface of the ground it is attracted to, depends upon the nature of that body, over and beyond the fact of its mass and trajectory. Gravity serves as condition, to which its range of activity is subject, but in no way exhaustively determines that activity. Of course, other laws apply, and not just anything can fly; it is, in the end, only the combined impact of all such conditions that determine a body's movements. The key thing to note, that makes such determination compatible with at least the possibility of freedom, is that the total set of conditions, and the decisive factors for action, include factors Plato attributes to the soul, that which gives life to the living body: its perceptions and desires, emotions, and thoughts.

Obviously, we can't escape gravity, as Alex surely knows when he leaps from a window, expecting to die. We can't breathe water. We can't go back in time, or become other than human. Whether he wants to or not, Alex will never fulfill his fantasy of being a Roman centurion, as he imagines while reading the Bible, or a vampire, as he imagines while masturbating to Beethoven.

So perhaps we should modify the definition to mean the capacity to follow one's inclinations, without any constraints other than the bounds of natural possibilities. Prison walls and Ludovico treatments are unnatural, and so go against freedom. Someone with a crippling disease, however, is not unfree just because by nature he can't do what others can. This is a bit tricky, since the writer can't walk and presumably he'd like to. In one sense, the constraint is natural, since his legs no longer function. The impetus, though, was Alex, who'd kicked him down the stairs. He wouldn't say he wasn't free, just that he can no longer do all the things that he might like. What keeps us from saying the same of Alex – that the impact of his treatment is he simply can no longer do the

violent things he used to like? He's no longer imprisoned. The constraints are inside him, his feelings and reactions. Unlike the writer, who
never had a chance against Alex and his droogs, Alex chose the treatment as an alternative to imprisonment. He may not have understood
the consequences, but we rarely know what will result from or happen
to us as a result of our actions, and, even when our actions constrain us,
we still, usually, think ourselves as free.

Alex, we can say, still wants to be violent, but the thought of it sickens him, and the sickening is overpowering. Compare this with, say,
another who would like to hurt someone but is sickened by the thought
because he thinks it would be wrong. If he doesn't do it, it is because his
sense of right and wrong wins out over his inclination to do harm.
Obviously, we might think, he's free. Then, however, let's imagine that
this sense of right and wrong developed over many years of painful
"education" on the part of cruel and dogmatic parents and teachers.
He'd like to disobey them, but has internalized their cruelty in the form
of feelings of self-loathing that arise within him on the occasions he
considers acting otherwise than in accordance with their edicts. Is it still
so obvious he's free? The differences between this case and that of Alex
after treatment seem nothing more than subtleties.

To go further, we might compare this case and that of Alex with that
of an apparently ordinary person, someone who occasionally has strong
urges she doesn't follow because they simply don't feel right. If we suppose, reasonably, that her inclinations and urges as well as her feelings
for what is right and wrong are heavily influenced by her parents and
teachers and by things she's seen and read, it is hard to see how she
would be essentially different either. If the others aren't free, it is hard to
see how she would be. If she is, it is hard to say why they're not. We
might say the difference is in the strength of the opposing feelings. Alex
can't help but succumb, but for the ordinary person her urges sometimes
overcome her feeling that it's wrong. In that case, though, when her
urges win out, it doesn't seem to be a win for freedom. We'd expect her
to say, in that case, that she wanted to do the right thing but she
couldn't help it: her urge was too strong. She might resist saying that
she wasn't free, but might instead say that she was powerless. The
difference, here, does seem no more than semantics.

We sometimes identify freedom with the will, with what we want to
do, whether we do it or don't. When the will is overpowered, though,
we shouldn't then say it was free. If other urges have the power to
obstruct the will on occasion, it would be odd to say it is free only when
it happens to win. So if the will is what we want to do, and we only
occasionally do what we want, we'd have to say that the will is not free.

Better to say there are many inclinations competing within us, urges and feelings, drives and motivations, but the one we identify with is what we say we want, understanding that this is not always decisive for how we end up acting. If I feel hungry, and there are no other, stronger, urges at work in me than the desire to eat, I will and will say I did what I wanted. If I'm hungry for a cookie, and I'm trying to diet, I might eat it anyway and blame it on weakness. In both cases we'd tend to say I was free, but in the latter that I'd made a poor choice, done what I didn't really want to do. We, ordinarily, think of ourselves as free as long as what drives us is in us, whether we end up doing what we wanted to or not. We wouldn't generally say we're not free unless what prevents us from what we want is something outside of us, such as prison bars or a gun to the head.

What makes Alex's situation seem so much different is that he identifies with his urges to inflict violence; he wants to inflict violence, but has overwhelming feelings that prevent him. These feelings are internal now, but were implanted in him by means of the treatment. As we've seen, however, this is not so far from anyone, whose feelings and inclinations come to them from their culture or their background, or even their biology or psychology, none of which they chose at all. Where they do have choices to follow this or that influence, they are just as likely to have been influenced there as well. If that's so, it may be a mistake to say we're ever free. If, even prior to his treatment, Alex was acting on compulsions he'd acquired as a result of the combination of his psychological makeup, his parental influence (or lack thereof), and cultural and artistic influences, then we shouldn't say that even then he was free. If I act as I want, but what I want is constrained or controlled by influences out of my control, then my so-called freedom turns out to be empty.

We might avoid the conclusion we're never truly free, if we consider that not all influences are contrary to our interests. As Socrates never fails to insist, no one acts willingly against his own interests. If he does what goes against them, it is because he doesn't know what is good for him. Perhaps being free is just a matter of knowing and pursuing what is truly in one's interests. Perhaps freedom is only truly available to those who learn to look beyond appearances, to overcome the associations and habits that shape their inclinations, and become able to act not in accordance with prejudice but according to insights into what is best. A genuine freedom, as Plato's work suggests, only comes to those who break free of the chains that bind them in the cave, rejecting the opinions that keep them set in their ways, and begin to pursue the life of inquiry, the life of philosophy.

In the early part of the *Republic*, Socrates is speaking with Thrasymachus, who argues that what we call justice is just whatever serves the interests of the ruling class, or, in other words, that might makes right. Socrates reminds him that rulers make mistakes, and points out that what they do can't serve their interests if they don't know what those interests are. All the power they possess can only make them miserable – against their wills – if they merely act upon impulses that don't truly serve them. Towards the end of the book, he examines the psychology of the tyrant, to show that what looks like the most perfect kind of freedom – the power of one to rule over all – amounts in fact to nothing more than enslavement to the tyranny of one's many desires. It's worth taking a look at his portrait of the tyrant, because it resembles closely the picture of Alex developed in *A Clockwork Orange*.

We all, according to Socrates, have desires incompatible with society and with law. In most of us these are kept in check by our better desires and our awareness of the rule of law. We become aware of them when they manifest in sleep, in dreams, when the wild part inside of us

> dares to do everything as though it were released from, and rid of, all shame and prudence. And it doesn't shrink from attempting intercourse, as it supposes, with a mother or with anyone else at all – human beings, gods, and beasts, or attempting any foul murder at all, and there is no food from which it abstains. And, in a word, it omits no act of folly or shamelessness.
>
> (571c–d)

Those who are healthy and moderate nourish their thinking, first of all, by considering the reasons why one ought to behave well, but are sure also to take care that their other desires are satisfied, so that neither hunger, lust, nor anger disrupt their sleep. The tyrant, by contrast, seeks to impose his dreamed desires upon his waking life. Those who have grown up to despise the lawfulness and moderation in the society around them and especially in their parents, who consider their moderation a weakness and form of servitude, are predisposed to enjoy the company of those who flatter them and encourage them in vices. They'll take advantage of their parents' weaknesses, they'll learn to flatter those with power, and lord it over those who are weaker. The portrait is not exact in all of its details, but in outline resembles Alex well, whose waking visions, dreams, and reality as depicted in the film are very much as Socrates describes.

If, by some ill fate, such a person gains power in the city, it would appear from far away as if it were the greatest kind of freedom. As a matter of fact, the tyrant has no true friends, and will always need to look out that those who surround him don't get the upper hand – just as Alex attempted but failed to do with his droogs, who allowed him to be caught as soon as they had the chance to do so without his retaliation. He is forced to flatter those he considers his inferiors – as Alex flatters his probationary officer and parents – and sometimes offer them great rewards in exchange for not turning against him. Even on his own, in the absence of the kind of power which puts his life in constant danger, the tyrannical person is content only so long as he is able to pursue his various and voracious desires, which usually requires that he steal from others, continuously putting himself at risk and making enemies of both friends and strangers.

Alex's cure: freedom and philosophy

The only one who truly lives well, and is content, according to Socrates, is the one whose interests coincide with what in fact is for the best, and are consistent with the well-being of those around him. Early on in the *Republic*, he distinguishes between three major motivating drives within each of us: desire, spirit, and reason. Health, within the soul, consists of harmony between these, and this harmony is what he considers real justice. We all, to varying degrees, have desires for food, drink, and sex, and we care about money because it gives power to secure most of the rest. Each of us, likewise, has a sense of personal dignity, a sense of honor or spiritedness that leads us to take offense and fight back when we are insulted, and to take pride when we are honored and respected. Finally, each of us has an innate curiosity about how things work and how to work things; we like to know, we'd prefer not to be ignorant. While all of us care about all of these things, most people care most of all about one or the other; most identify most strongly with just one of these various drives. Some are motivated, above all, by considerations of money or of sex, or at least seek, above all, for material comforts. Others care more that they are "making a difference" or that they are accomplishing something that is considered honorable or respectable or that they be recognized for courageous actions in the field of duty. Others, though fewer, care most about knowing, about getting things right rather than achieving recognition for being persuasive.

According to Socrates, each way of life and each kind of pursuit is pleasurable, and yet the pleasures of desire and honor are always mixed with pain unless they are also accompanied by wisdom. The one who pursues only lusts, without honor, without concern or care for those harmed, may manage to seduce through his lies, but will never be satisfied. The pursuit of honor is fraught with risk, and when power and honor are treated as ends in themselves, their pursuer nearly always ends up making enemies. Enduring satisfactions accompany the pursuit of wisdom, and the wise person seeks out honor only in pursuits she deems honorable, and pursues desires honorably. It is not that the others do not want to be happy, but that they pursue what can only bring a moment's satisfaction. Alex thought that by assailing his droogs after they'd asked for their fair share of the spoils of their robberies, by knocking them into the water and then slicing George across the hand, that he was ensuring their respect. In fact, he was earning their resentment, which led to their turning upon him, and ended up landing him in jail. His incautious and unwise pursuit of his desires, for sex and money, but above all for power, led directly to his becoming powerless, first in jail, then strapped to a chair, and finally wretching at the very thought of defending himself. What seemed to be his final act, throwing himself out the window, was the only power he had then to retain whatever sense of honor and dignity in him remained.

That he did not die, however, and lived to tell his tale, seems to be something of a victory. Certainly he tells his story that way. "I jumped, oh my brothers, and I fell hard, but I did not snuff it," he speaks as the camera tracks from his feet across his entire body, in a full body cast, with bandages on his head. "If I had snuffed it, I would not be here to tell what I've told now. I came back to life after a long, black, black gap, what might have been a million years." That the blackness he refers to was just a moment for us, a brief fade to black following a quick, kinetic falling shot as if from his plummeting point of view, reminds us that what we've seen so far has (for the most part) been his story, as he sees it. By the end, he'll have his enemies beneath him, his parents begging his forgiveness, and the Minister his ally, now cured and able to pursue his interests as he sees fit, all with the sanction of the government. We might recall here as well a popular gloss on the suggestions of Thrasymachus – who argued early on in the *Republic* that might makes right – that the victors write the history books.

He's visited by his "P and M," who've had a change of heart after reading the new headlines, which now depict Alex as the unfortunate victim of government scientists. His father ("P"), now remorseful, suggests they shared in the blame; his mother ("M") weeps, as Alex tells them they're no longer welcome. A psychologist comes to visit him next. He questions her about a strange dream in which doctors were "messing around inside my gulliver," suggesting vague memories of a new treatment, which had, apparently, been successful. When she asks him to fill in the blanks in a kind of cartoon Rorschach test, his playful but disturbing responses establish beyond doubt that he's no longer averse to thoughts of violence and sex.

The real test comes next, when the Minister himself arrives, and explains it was all an unfortunate mistake. They'd listened to the wrong people and an inquiry he's ordered will decisively place the blame on someone else. They've taken care of Alex, ensuring him the best of care following his unfortunate accident. "You see," he says, as he spoon feeds him from a hospital tray, "we are looking out for your interests. We are interested in you." He'll be given a generous salary and an interesting job in exchange for, well, "helping us." "It is no secret that this government has lost a lot of popularity because of you, my boy .... The press has chosen to take a very unfavorable view of what we tried to do. But, public opinion has a way of changing, and you, Alex ... can be instrumental in changing the public's verdict." He looks at him pointedly, "Do you understand, Alex? Do I make myself clear?" "As an unmuddied lake, Fred, as clear as an azure sky of deepest summer. You can rely on me, Fred," he replies; and the Minister, smiling, tells him he has what he hopes will be a welcome surprise for Alex, a symbol of their newfound understanding and mutually beneficial friendship. Beethoven's Ninth now begins to play as his assistants roll in a pair of very large speakers and a stereo system, and the press arrives to capture candid snapshots of Alex and the Minister, mugging and hugging and signing an enthusiastic thumbs up as the music blasts around them.

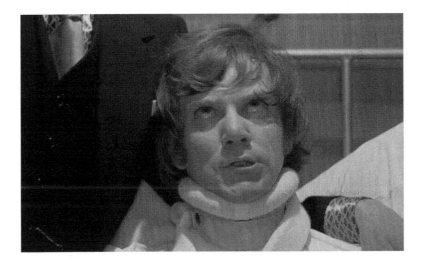

The frame returns us to the face of Alex, now not looking at us or at anything visible. He sees, rather, what isn't there, what he only imagines. It is a look of helpless bliss, one we've seen before, as when Alex looked up from the Bible in the prison library and imagined himself a centurion whipping Christ, or a Hebrew soldier lounging with concubines after a fierce battle. Or when, following a night out with his droogs, he returned home to masturbate in bed, listening to Beethoven while contemplating his portrait, and imagined himself a vampire presiding over scenes of horror. If to see a face is to see what sees, to see this face is to see that it doesn't see. At least, it isn't looking at anything that anyone else could look upon. It is a private gaze, which signals daydream or a fantasy. Eyes glazed over, eyeballs elevated, his mouth drooping stupidly, he's no longer even aware of our gaze or of the look of the reporters taking his picture with the Minister. A moment before, he'd been mugging for the camera, one arm around the Minister, both smiling with thumbs up. Now, as Beethoven's "Ode to Joy" reaches its glorious peak, the camera zooms in to frame his face tightly and his smile contorts into a rapturous, orgasmic gaze, a gaze that sees what isn't there where we imagine him to be.

And yet, we do see what he imagines. The frame reveals to us his fantasy. He's lying on his back, naked in a bed of fake snow, while a beautiful blond woman, completely nude, twists and turns astride him in slow motion as he grips her by the hips to secure her in place. An admiring crowd looks on and applauds. As she struggles to escape and as the symphony concludes, he gives himself the final word: "I was cured, all right," and the credits roll to Gene Kelly's own exuberant rendition of "Singin' in the Rain."

The distinction, in this case, between what is real and just imagined, is easily discerned. He's there, in the hospital bed, surrounded by reporters, the Minister beside him; he imagines the woman, the crowd, and the applause. We see his face, smiling at the reporters; as the camera zooms in, his eyes roll upwards, and we see that he no longer sees anything. When the frame then cuts to show us Alex in the snow, we know it is not anything he sees directly from the room and it is not something happening afterwards, but perhaps after he'd recovered from the injuries that currently have him in a full body cast. If there were any doubt about that, the fact that the frame shifts back and forth between this image and the image of his face lets us know that this is not something happening later, but is what is happening then, not in the same room but in his imagination. Before considering directly the meaning of this final fantasy, let's return now to the theme of imagination generally and its relation to ordinary experience.

Of course, as we've seen, everything on screen is in some sense imagined. That's not to say it isn't real, but that it isn't anything for us unless we entertain its moments as interconnected and related. We need to link moments together, identifying objects that endure throughout change, and discern at least to some degree a pattern to that change. The same is true, in fact, of everyday experience, of everything we know or learn regarding "reality itself." Experience makes sense because it hangs together, and it hangs together because we hold it together. To make sense of what is on screen, in particular, we need to remember what has come before and anticipate what is coming next. We need to compare what we're seeing now with what else we've seen, to respond to cues allowing us to decipher the sequence of events and decide how they hang together in an imagined time and space. In particular, we need to be able to respond to clues that what we're seeing is not a part of the reality being depicted, but a dream or a flashback or a fantasy sequence.

What we see on screen must be imagined because it can't be seen all at once, and because the time in which we imagine the events to unfold does not coincide with the time in which we experience the film. We can consider this entire imagined sequence, presented in the film, as the filmic reality, what the film presents as happening or as having happened. We can say of certain elements of the cinematic experience that they don't belong to that "reality," but that they nevertheless shape our sense of what it means and how it matters. The soundtrack, for example, may or may not present itself as part of the "happenings" depicted on screen. It is, nevertheless, part of our experience of the film, and shapes for us the meaning of that experience. Depictions of dreams or fantasies or even flashbacks on film are like that, too, insofar as they offer insight into how the characters interpret and experience their situations. We usually have little trouble distinguishing the filmic reality from its depictions of mere fantasy or subjective illusions. This dream sequence, for example, isn't part of the reality within which Alex's story unfolds, but is marked off from that reality as his purely private fantasy.

The sense in which we say Alex imagines, here in the closing scene or in the library or in his bedroom, is thus different from the general sense in which all experience is imaginative. What he imagines isn't real, which is to say it doesn't belong to the world that we imagine him to share with the Minister and the reporters and his parents and his former friends. It isn't something they can see, unless they imagine it too. The difference between what we imagine regarding Alex and his world as we make sense of the film, and what he imagines here according to the film, is that what we imagine is shared, by anyone who sees the film, or at least anyone who pays attention. Our imagined experience of the film is rooted in evidence, the evidence of the film itself, available to anyone who watches the film; and if anyone doubts whether, say, Alex said this or that, or did this or that, they can just watch the movie and check. By contrast, no one else in Alex's world is privy to his private imaginations. They share his experience, insofar as they witness the same world. His imagination is private, except insofar as to watch the film is to imagine that we share it with him.

This contrast, however, between a purely private imaginative experience and the everyday experience shared with others, should not be drawn too sharply, and this film itself calls it into question. Alex shares a world with others, but his experience of events, as it is depicted in this film, differs sharply from what those others experience. Consider, for example, the contrast between Alex's experience of his home invasion – as a kind of performance artwork – and that same event of terror as experienced by the writer and his wife. The difference owes something to differing vantage points, and, obviously, to the fact that Alex and his droogs are perpetrators and the writer and his wife are the victims. At the same time, the contrast was, as we've seen, communicated to us by way of a difference in the style and approach of the camera, a difference that emphasized for us that Alex conceived his act as a musical number, while the writer and his wife were simply shocked and overwhelmed by the incongruity between his violent actions and what was, for them, the chaos of his improvised song and dance.

How events are experienced results from the activity of imagination, which gives us the capacity to retain, recall, invent, compare, and arrange images, even when they are no longer presently available to be sensed. Experience thus amounts to a preliminary interpretation of events, which, when elaborated upon and verbalized or depicted becomes a story, a narrative. The same situations and the same encounters can give rise to different experiences, which would then be narrated differently: "We came across a filthy dirty old drunky, howling away at the filthy songs of his fathers and going blurb blurp in between as it might be a filthy old orchestra in his rotten, stinking gut" could just as well have been "We came across a destitute old man who had apparently been drinking, and was singing an old Irish folk song." The differences are not in the facts, but in their significance, and carry with them different moral implications. To experience the man as Alex does is to see the man's presence as an abomination, to which their subsequent actions seem an appropriate response. A different experience of the same situation would solicit a very different response.

That is not to say that how things are experienced is purely make-believe. Our manner of making sense of things develops out of real encounters, sharable by others, but arranged and considered in ways that vary from person to person, based on different backgrounds, assumptions, and interests. This is exactly what Socrates meant to suggest in relating the allegory of the cave, that we are not in contact with reality itself, but with its shadows. Now the preliminary interpretations we make of events, and stories we tell others and ourselves regarding what has happened, tend to coincide in their details. We are seeing the same shadows, after all. Where interpretations tend to differ is in the emphases we place on those "facts," in the ways we arrange them to give them a significance that connects up with our interests. We can't, though, avoid interpretation. To stick with "just the facts" requires a highly cultivated attitude – that of science or of law, for example – in which we step back from our specific interests and assess our situations based on shared standards.

The only standard Alex appears to accept is a subjective one, however, which means he's firmly trapped in the depths of the cave, facing the shadows, ignoring the light. He measures all situations in terms of whether or not they conform to his interests. He attempts to impose his interpretations on others, just as the prisoners did to each other in Plato's allegory, and in particular the film presents him as telling his story to us, the audience, in a way that will win us to his ways of seeing things. He encourages his audience to become interested in his interests, to care that he will succeed. In that sense, the difference between his current fantasy and the overall story he tells himself and others as he construes his activities and encounters is not as sharp as it initially seemed. Both are imaginary constructs rooted in his life encounters, but the fantasy is to a greater degree unhinged from the specifics of his situation that are available to others as well.

Yet because his fantasies are unhinged from the world he shares with others, they reveal more directly his interests, which also shape his interpretations of the situations he lives through. His final fantasy, in fact, suggests an overall interpretation of his experiences that we should consider more closely. He has told us his story, which is to say that the film presents him as telling us his story. It is, as he tells it, a kind of riches to rags to riches tale. It is the story of how he went from being on top of his world, leader of his own gang, to being jailed and, as he has it, used and abused by the system, to the point where he attempts suicide, but is finally cured and is once again on top of the world. The final scene is meant to demonstrate his triumphant overcoming of the difficulties that had faced him.

This concluding image is both arousing and unsettling, a perfect image of the power of images, which manage to captivate audiences as they violate their minds. It is hard to know exactly what it means: a well-dressed audience applauds as Alex lies down in the snow and holds down an undressed and struggling woman on top of him. It could be symbolic, representing Alex's fantasy of the public's acceptance and encouragement of his sexual aggression; or it could suggest a kind of wedding, where the well-heeled crowd stand as witnesses to its forced consummation. In either case, the image is at once exciting and awful, simultaneously erotic and disgusting. It's staged to be aesthetically pleasing, but its subject matter is troubling. The music celebrates joy and triumph, its words a paean to the reconciliation of brothers and sisters, to the overcoming of enmity. Their combination is profoundly troubling and ambiguous. The woman is on top, in a position that signals sexual mastery and control, a position that suggests consent, when in fact she is helpless, held down, attempting to escape as she is being raped. There is no reconciliation here, only forced union. At the same time, the presence of the audience, dressed up in vintage garb and clapping enthusiastically, suggests that all of this may be just a performance, that the woman may be merely acting out a fantasy, and there is a hint that her struggle is insincere, that it is insufficiently vigorous. If it is merely a performance, it might be considered analogous to the performance of the woman who, following Alex's treatment, was hired by the government to come on stage naked in order to entice the audience and tempt Alex. Now, that feeling, that she may not really want to escape, that her struggle is pretend, may be no more than a rapist's self-delusional perception, and we are reminded once again that this is Alex's fantasy, and that, as he perceives it, all women he's attracted to are natural subjects for rape. At the same time, to witness this image is to share in that fantasy, is to wonder about the sincerity of precisely her desire to escape.

This concluding image, of an oxymoronic "consensual rape," however inappropriate and unseemly it seems, turns out to be highly appropriate as an image for what moving images and media can perpetrate on their all-too-willing audiences. As the Minister knows, public opinions are easily manipulated. The film shows specifically the way that Alex's own parents have their minds determined about him by the headlines in the current papers. The Minister's words echo those of the writer, who opposes him, suggesting a perpetual wisdom that drives all political parties, the real masters of the shadow play that forms consensus among the many. Upon encountering Alex in the rain, and before he knew who it really was, the writer had called up his allies to tell them what an opportunity this presented. He tells them that the common people "must be led, driven, pushed" to defend their so-called "liberties," and they can be so led when the press is manipulated into telling stories that earn their outrage. Now, as the Minister assures Alex, the writer is out of the picture, where he can no longer do him harm, but the veiled threat that appears not to escape Alex entirely is that a very real potential for harm remains in the hands of the government, which will do whatever it takes to remain on top.

When Alex concludes his narration with the claim that he was cured, he means, obviously, that he no longer feels sick at the thought of inflicting violence. He was cured of the cure, cured of the conditioning that Doctors Branom and Brodsky had assured would make him healthy, would lead him to "respond to the presence of the hateful with fear and nausea." Yet, his final vision suggests something more than simply the return to his prior lusts. His fantasy is more precise, a fantasy of rape that can seem to be consensual, and that is thereby applauded and accepted by a well-heeled audience. This new form of fantasy suggests that his "cure" includes an insight into the nature of the political domain. He'd already seen, at first incredulous, that George and Dim are now policemen, part of the system that they'd once considered against them. He sees now, clearly, how the Minister manipulates facts, twisting them to serve his own political aims – and that the opposition party did the same. He's come to see that what really matters in the political realm is not doing what is right, but convincing the public that you're right, and pinning your wrongs upon a convenient scapegoat. In other words, he's learned the lesson of Thrasymachus, that might makes right, and that those who manipulate the media most effectively control thereby the minds and affections of the masses. Whereas the Ludovico treatment was to teach him to hate what is hateful, what he has now learned is that power gives the power to define what is hateful and what can be celebrated. His final cure, then, amounts to a kind of education, which allows him to see eye to eye with the Minister – and they're now on first-name basis – and manipulate the system for his personal and private gain.

At the same time, the image that epitomizes his triumphant insight is more subtle than he may know, or may seem to us at first. He considers himself victorious, but it is only in his mind. His freedom is merely a fantasy, unhinged from the reality he shares with others, precisely because he fails to acknowledge the legitimacy of viewpoints that differ from his own, or of standards higher than his personal satisfaction. We see the political context that allows him to feel triumphant and free, but in fact ensures the limits to that freedom. The film had shown us the newspaper headlines, which had previously celebrated the government's new approach to crime, but now condemned it for injustices against Alex. We can see that the government is on his side, but only insofar as doing so can turn the news in its favor, only as long as it can use him to win the support of popular opinion. He imagines himself applauded by the public for actions he once had to perform with a mask, but he fails to see that now he is under the public eye he will have only the latitude allowed to him by that public. It is not so much that he will be applauded for his actions but, rather, that – as celebrities learn quite quickly – he will be allowed to act only as long as those actions receive applause.

We see not only the image, but see him imagining it. The image of his face, as he imagines his victory, is far from the look of self-assured mastery with which the film began. It resembles nothing so much as helpless bliss, the mirror image of the look of abject terror on the face of the writer while his wife was being raped, and his subsequent helpless rapture as he tortured Alex in his attic with the booming sounds of Beethoven. Alex, his face now fixed in a state of orgiastic bliss, has his body bound, immobile, in a complete body cast, and is helpless, unable even to feed himself. He'll recover from that, perhaps, but will retain his current status as poster boy for the government only as long as they remain in power and he continues to serve their interests. His education is, in fact, incomplete, as he imagines that the Minister who is, for the moment, willing to feed him, and whom he playfully humiliates by opening his mouth wide and eager for each next bite, will remain standing by his side when the news cycle shifts, and he is no longer needed as a pawn for their popularity. So the image we see is not merely that of his triumphant "cure," but of him helpless, bound, in bed, spoon-fed by the government, existing only at their mercy, and yet imagining himself free. Perhaps we should consider, paradoxically, that Alex, who considers himself to be on top, is the one who is unwittingly manipulated, raped, by the regime, while the public looks on, applauding.

So Alex thinks he's been punished sufficiently, and learned the true lesson, which is, ironically, what the Minister had claimed was the only lesson prison teaches as he extolled the superior benefits of the Ludovico treatment. Prison, he'd said, teaches "the false smile, the rubbed hands of hypocrisy, the fawning greased obsequious leer." It teaches, in other words, that what matters is not what you are or what you do, but how you appear to others, the very lesson that he so effectively teaches Alex as he recruits his assistance in modifying his party's public image. He'd argued, against the "old way," that punishment is useless, what was needed was a cure for criminality, which would not only make the criminal seem better but be better, by learning to loathe lawlessness. In fact, though, the whole scheme turned out to be nothing more than a political ploy to win public support, and the political ploy backfired.

Socrates, likewise, insists in the *Republic* that punishment is useless and unjust. If to punish is to harm, then punishment, as the Minister also notes, serves only to make a bad person worse. The only proper penalty for the one who acts badly is education, but not an education in hypocrisy. Rather, an education that amounts to a turning around of the soul away from the ideas that rule here down in the cave: that consensus is the mark of truth, and that power is the mark of justice. As we have seen, true education is not at all a matter of installing information in the mind of the ignorant. It consists, rather, of asking questions that confront the learner with her own ideas and values, and encourage her to become unsettled in her attitudes and habits. The true education encourages the learner to develop the habit of inquiry, and the willingness to follow the path that appears to stand up to scrutiny and turns out to be best upon examination, rather than the one that seems initially convincing. One does not learn to be satisfied with appearances, as long as they're widely accepted or have authority on their side. The true education is an education in freedom, because it involves learning how to release oneself from the bonds of one's own prejudice and from the chains of popular opinion. True freedom is not the power of the tyrant to follow inclinations acquired as a result of immoderate behavior. True freedom is not the spontaneous capacity to make an unmotivated choice among arbitrary alternatives, because we are never fully free from external and internal motivations. True freedom comes, rather, from the acquired capacity to discern what is at stake in the various conflicting urges and attitudes that drive us, and develop the discipline to respond appropriately, to pursue what is truly good and worthwhile, to see the shadows as shadows and turn toward the light.

Conclusion
Shadow philosophy

> The fundamental condition of art, therefore, is that we shall be distinctly conscious of the unreality of the artistic production, and that means that it must be absolutely separated from real things and men, that it must be isolated and kept in its own sphere. As soon as a work of art tempts us to take it as a piece of reality, it has been dragged into the sphere of practical action ... Its completeness in itself is lost, and its value for our aesthetic enjoyment has faded away.
>
> (Hugo Münsterberg, *Hugo Münsterberg on Film*, p. 123)

Turning toward the light, as we've seen, doesn't involve going someplace else. It is not a matter of turning away from life, escaping one's time and immersing oneself in the pursuit alone of timeless truths, or of ignoring all that's popular, such as television and the movies. Even popular art forms, such as cinema, have the potential to provoke philosophical inquiry. It is in their likeness to life that they encourage us to reflect on it. It is in their difference from life that they create a distance, allowing us to confront directly and examine the prejudices and assumptions regarding everyday life and experience that we ordinarily take for granted.

The philosophy born from investigating cinema does not develop as a result of turning away from the shadows, but of learning to see them differently. When we go to the movies, we are confronted with shadows, just like those that make up our everyday life, but these shadows reveal themselves as such. The mistake of Plato's prisoners is not that they consider the shadows to be real, but that they fail to see through them to the conditions that generate them. They are real but dependent realities, and to see them rightly is to recognize that what they are and how they appear is the result of conditions that exceed them. The images of cinema are more obviously artificial, dependent upon artists and technicians and a highly skilled industry, all employed in an effort to create captivating motion pictures. Yet we often fail to follow up on the provocations they offer to reconsider our grasp on the realities they resemble.

The awareness, always implicit as part of the experience of watching movies, that what we are witnessing is not real, but may be thought to approximate reality in some way or other, already indicates a first inescapable dimension of cinematic intelligibility, and thereby a space wherein philosophical thinking can take root. There is, to be specific, a threefold tension at work in the cinematic experience. To witness a motion picture is, first, to encounter something real, even if it is nothing more than a moving play of shadows and light, and this encounter calls upon the same perceptual capacities we employ in our experience of everyday life. It is, however, manifestly unreal, set apart from those realities we interact with day to day. At the same time, and this is the aspect emphasized when the film is considered as an image, what is encountered on screen is seen to resemble something real, something it isn't. What this means is that the experience of watching movies operates already with a number of distinctions, whose implications and applications philosophy can clarify and explore. There is the idea of a reality, or of the way things really are; there is the idea of an appearance and of a difference between appearance and reality; there is, further, the idea of resemblance or copy. Similar distinctions appear in our experience of other kinds of images and artworks, such as photographs and paintings, except that the perception of these tends to lack the immersive character of the screen experience, which enables the rest of reality to largely fade into the background.

Cinema is, nevertheless, distinctive not only for its immersive character, its ability to draw us in almost completely so that the rest of reality disappears into the darkness of the theater. It draws upon the imagination, as do literature and other art forms, and yet it gives a determinacy to the objects we imagine in the space the film depicts, that allows the activity of imagination to feel more like a passive apprehension. What is more, what is imagined in the cinema is, for the most part, something shared with the rest of the audience. Even where some may disagree regarding what they see, the film can be repeated and discussed together, in order to clarify and complicate what was seen in an initial viewing. The filmic presentation unfolds according to its own inexorable time, which overlaps with the time of our own experience and is nevertheless not reducible to it. Film operates directly with and upon our memory and anticipation, calling upon us to make sense of its presentation, and at the same time leading us to care how things come out. None of these features – its immersive character and vividness, its temporality and ability to draw upon and manipulate the audience's sense of time, its narrative dimension, which requires interpretation and solicits care, its capacity for repetition and intersubjective confirmation – are unique to cinema, but it is arguably distinctive in the way it is able to draw upon all of these features to generate in audiences a shared and discussible temporal experience of a reality like but distinct from their lives with characters and outcomes and events they care about and need to make sense of.

These features allow cinema to interrupt everyday experience, unfolding in ways that form a state of exception from our usual expectations, that calls upon us to hold at least some of these assumptions at bay and may draw upon others in order to later call them into question. Film allows us to entertain and even find convincing for a time possibilities that we need not assert or accept. In its contrast and linkage with situations and ways of being we do judge to be real or right, the cinema pushes us to consider what it means to make this judgment. It allows us to compare and check our intuitions regarding such questions, makes it possible to deliver detailed analyses of the filmic presentation, which can be shared and appraised, and can stimulate discussion.

The suggestion, in brief, is to consider the experience of cinema as an expanded variation on the allegory of the cave. It is as if each film has the potential to offer a glimpse into the inner workings of the cave, a detailed depiction of actual shadow plays the prisoners might be said to witness. Plato employed the allegory to encourage reflection on ordinary experience in the absence of philosophy, and to highlight thereby the nature of philosophical thinking. The allegory has been used here to clarify the multiple dimensions of cinema (audience, apparatus, film) by means of which meaning comes to light. The experience of cinema, the experience of watching movies – understood as an encounter between audience, apparatus and film – can at the same time serve to build upon and expand the allegory, giving it a richness unglimpsed in its initial rendering. On the one hand, it reminds us that experience generally draws upon each of these moments – there is an object only for a subject, and only under certain conditions, both material and ideal. At the same time, each film operates within and allows us to explore the conditions of cinematic intelligibility, and to learn something thereby about the intelligibility of everyday life. Of course, in the terms of the allegory, we are ourselves the prisoners, but in the case of cinema we have a distinct advantage over the prisoners, which is that on some level, and even in the absence of any advanced philosophical training, we know that what we witness is not real, is merely appearance, and is artificial, the product of artifice.

Cinematic experience is a part of life, at least for most of us in the modern world, and yet it is also set apart from everyday life. Audience awareness of that difference, between what they experience on screen and what they encounter otherwise, implies a tacit critical dimension to cinema that is not present for the prisoners in Plato's cave. That is to say that the cinematic experience naturally solicits appraisal on the part of the audience, even if this critical appraisal remains for the most part underdeveloped, and remains largely implicit and unspoken. There are at least four interrelated critical lines of questioning that arise naturally from cinema, and each of these opens the space for further critical assessment. Each film is different and its provocations specific, which means that the pathways for thinking each offers can only be spelled out in the course of detailed and close analyses, but at least some of the range of possible philosophical questions provoked by reflections on cinema can be hinted at in what follows.

Reality (metaphysics)

There is, first, what we might call the reality question. To be engaged in the work, to have it work on them in ways analogous to their experience of everyday life, audiences must find at least some of what they see on screen plausible. It must be able to hang together for them as an imagined reality. Otherwise, as we say, they are unable to suspend disbelief. It feels too artificial for them to care. To really work, a film needs to win audience conviction – they need to believe in the characters, on some level at least, and care about some of them some of the time at least somewhat. Now, there are whole genres of film, such as science fiction or fantasy, which exhibit elements we know to be impossible or unlikely. Yet we can imagine such things, and having established the terms for what kinds of things to expect, we expect that the rest will conform to our sense of what could be. A superhero might fly, but he ought to say things consistent with his character. An audience can be drawn out from their immersion within the film experience as much when a sympathetic live-action talking dog falls for an implausibly obnoxious, coiffured canine as when an ordinary woman does something she couldn't because it would violate the spatio-temporal continuity established in the film to that point.

This tension in the cinematic experience – between the reality of the moving image, its distinction from the rest of reality, and its resemblance to something it isn't – isn't merely something we discover when we analyze the experience from a position outside of it, as objective observers. It is a tension that is, we might say, constitutive of or intrinsic to the cinematic experience, and accounts for specific features of that experience. If an audience member, for example, were not aware that what she witnessed was unreal, she would react and respond to it differently than film audiences tend do. Witnessing a murder on screen, she might exit the theater or call out for help, for example. If it didn't resemble reality at all, however, and didn't elicit a perceptual and emotional response at least akin to that of a real-life murder, she would feel nothing about it and would sit unmoved by the spectacle, or, more likely, would leave bored. She's supposed to care about the characters she sees on screen, to feel afraid and perhaps even scream; she's not supposed to run away and call the cops. To witness a murder on screen is to see something that makes us feel a certain way, while we know it isn't what it seems to be and therefore, rightly, fail to act upon those feelings.

Early film theorists, focused just on what appears on screen considered in abstraction from the overall experience of cinema, drew attention to a related tension, between the tendency of the filmic image to be lifelike, what we might call its realism, and its artificiality, its distance from reality, a tendency that theorists labeled formalism. Some argued that one of these aspects or the other was essential to cinema, its distinctive feature. Better to consider this an essential tension. Specific films can place emphasis on one or the other of these dimensions of the cinematic experience, but cannot efface the importance of the other. We've already seen in our discussion of the rape scene from *A Clockwork Orange* how effectively Kubrick exploits just this tension.

Realist films emphasize long takes, for example, such that actions unfold in real time; in doing so, however, they give the audience room to think, or to doze off, to feel their bodies in their chairs, reminding them of the distance between their ongoing, embodied experience and what unfolds on the screen. Or, realist films can employ handheld cameras, suggesting documentary-style capture of ephemeral events in the wild; but shaky camera work can become a style that precisely calls attention to the artificiality of events unfolding in the presence of a camera. Formalist films employ technical devices such as non-linear sequencing of events, but in doing so can work to bring audience attention closer to the experience they depict. Realist films employ stylistic devices in order to encourage audience conviction in what is being depicted. Formalist films highlight style and technique, in the service of aesthetics or the communication of distinctive ways of interpreting the subject matters they depict. At the same time, films like *A Clockwork Orange* draw upon both of these tendencies in order to highlight precisely the tension between reality and its representation on screen.

Formalist devices, such as those Kubrick employs in *A Clockwork Orange*, can give audiences a window onto subjectivities, into how things unfold from the perspective of a specific character. They give a sense for how things are felt or made sense of by the characters, and can also direct audiences to feel or think about them in specific ways. Realist films deliver the sense that what is seen on screen is objectively real – not in such a way as to efface the distinction between the reality and its representation, but to suggest that there is a reality captured by and shown through the representation. To say that it is real is, at least in part, to say that it is what it is regardless of how it is thought about. Realist devices, used effectively, suggest that what is seen is more than just an imitation of life because it captures and presents that life itself, or because it brings to life, and renders "real," what might otherwise be considered the unreality of a mere performance. Early formalist film theorists proposed that it was only the formal artistry of filmmakers that kept cinema from being merely mechanical recordings of independent realities that once were alive. Realist thinkers turned things around, worrying that too much (or the wrong kind of) artistry gave the impression of artifice. They suggested, by contrast, that the power of cinema lay precisely in its capacity to record and present – or create in the first place – ephemeral realities that pass away, and yet were autonomous in the sense of being irreducible to any given perception or interpretation of them. Realist artistry aimed to keep these ephemeral realities, these flowing passages of time, alive and vital, allowing them to maintain their impact and continue to speak to a variety of audiences over time.

Both traditions share a metaphysics, one that defines "reality" by way of a contrast with its image – whether that image is thought of as a representation or imitation or recording. At the same time, both suggest ways of surpassing that contrast, suggesting either that the image belongs to and has impact upon the "reality" it is considered to depict, or that "reality" itself, or what we take it to be, is itself merely an image. Formalist devices can complicate the contrast between image and reality, for example, by calling attention to the image itself, reminding audiences that what they're watching is merely a performance, that it is artificial and contrived. At the same time, these films can remind audiences that what they take for granted about everyday life is often also the product of manipulations and contrivances, and that we too easily overlook the fact that what we consider real is itself artificial and merely an appearance. Realist films, in their depictions of what seem to be autonomous realities, give us an opportunity and distance to begin to reflect upon and notice things we may never have considered, and in doing so they manage not only to reflect reality, but reshape it insofar as human beings are participants in that reality.

Nothing, in fact, is ever merely represented on film. Films accomplish something, they contribute to and transform the realities they reveal and depict. They do not merely represent reality, in other words, but participate in it. The twentieth-century German philosopher Martin Heidegger reflected upon the transformative power of Greek poetry in his seminal essay "The Origin of the Work of Art." He wrote:

> In the tragedy nothing is staged or displayed theatrically, but the battle of the new gods against the old is being fought. The linguistic work ... does not refer to this battle; it transforms the people's saying so that now every living word fights the battle and puts up for decision what is holy and what unholy, what great and what small, what brave and what cowardly, what lofty and what flighty, what master and what slave.
>   (Heidegger, "The Origin of the Work of Art," pp. 168–9)

All of that is just to say that the linguistic work – the tragedy, poem, novel, or epic – is actually a work, it works upon its readers, transforms them by giving them new ways of speaking and new ways of thinking that in fact reshape what for them are the possibilities of living together and being in the world. The same is true of cinema. Of course it may well be that some works of art – and many works of cinema – are largely derivative, operating within the ways of making sense and relating to the world already opened up and made possible by other works and by institutions and histories that precede them. Just as cinema can impact audiences in ways that confirm them in their prejudices, it can also transform their horizons so as to reshape their sense of who they are and ought to be and of what there is and of what matters.

In addition to provoking a variety of reflections regarding the tension between appearance and reality, or between representations and what they imitate, films naturally depict and enable exploration of a number of more specialized metaphysical considerations, such as the nature of identity and the possibility of freedom. Because the experience of cinema both shares in and gives shape to the experience of time undergone by its audience, film has a special affinity for and capacity to encourage reflection upon the temporal dimension of reality and experience. Some realist films, with their long takes that are experienced like real, lived time, can give a vivid sense for the duration and flow of everyday life, something we lose track of when we recall only significant events. Films can also make use of the flexibility of cinematic time to give an intuitive sense for complexities of narrative history, where one might say the past that remains real is only that which continues to impact the unfolding of the present.

Responsibility (ethics)

Audiences are always, at some level, asking whether what they see on screen is plausible, whether it could be real and how to make sense of it, and their answer to these questions decides the extent to which they are able to engage with what they encounter, perceptually and emotionally, in roughly the same way as they'd engage with everyday life. The fact that they at the same time know what they see to be disconnected from their everyday lives outside the theater means they don't feel compelled to interact with what they witness. Still, moviegoing is a part of their lives; it is something they do, and poses a second critical question: whether it is worth doing.

Going to the movies is a choice, and naturally raises the question whether it is choiceworthy. On the one hand, there's nothing special about cinema in this regard. Every choice we make – whether to get up in the morning, whether to go to school or work, whether to shop at a specific outlet and what to buy, whether and how to vote, whether to spend time with a friend or work out instead – every choice we make can be considered an answer to the question how we are and ought to live, what we value and why. Operating by habit, or according to popular opinion or prejudice, is a way of evading the question, operating as if the answer were obvious. The question is forced when what we encounter on screen goes against popular prejudice regarding morality, when (as did *A Clockwork Orange* at the time of its release) the film becomes a media scandal. Still, the question whether the content or approach of any particular film is ethical and the question whether watching movies is worthwhile are in principle distinct. Some films lead us to sympathize with characters we'd otherwise find morally repugnant, and it is a moral question whether that is problematic. What appears on screen may be unreal, but is an imitation of life, and evokes feelings real enough, and can shape and inform our attitudes and values whether for better or for worse. We've seen how Plato addresses related concerns in the *Republic*, as they apply not to film per se, but to storytelling generally.

Insofar as we come to care about the plights of characters on screen, we might sympathize with their actions. Our sympathies can, though, come into conflict with our moral intuitions otherwise. Films can bring us closer to people confronting unfamiliar situations, facing decisions we've never considered. Our assessments of their actions, and of their reasons for acting, can lead us to wonder whether our intuitions are correct, and thereby involve us in ethical reflections.

There is a close link between moral and aesthetic judgments. We often ask whether a given film was any good, and mean to ask about its quality as cinema. We want to know whether it was entertaining or boring, whether novel or derivative, whether the story was gripping or unconvincing and underdeveloped. What we really want to know, however, is whether it is worth our while or a waste of time. We ask whether it is *any* good, but what concerns us is whether it is *a* good, whether it improves upon the time it takes to watch it. However much it costs, these days, to buy a ticket to the movies, to see one is inevitably, also, to spend time in the theater, time that could be spent otherwise. A film might be entertaining – even a thrill ride – and yet feel empty, as if it had nothing to say, made no difference, felt a waste. Walking out of the cinema, after a film like that, we might consider it well made, and nevertheless think it would have been better had it never been made. Cinema, naturally, because it takes time, poses the question how best to spend it.

Interpretation (epistemology)

Those unwilling to accept the conventions of a genre film may find it difficult to engage with or find worth their while, whether as a story or as an experience. It won't win their conviction and won't earn their interest because they can't buy into its premises. Some can't do super-heroes, or Westerns, or musicals, or romantic comedies, or science fiction, or horror flicks. Some go into a film with expectations it can't sustain, or that its creators don't endorse. Some can't get into foreign or arthouse films. Subtitles scare some off. Films can be demanding. Good criticism and fair interpretation require preparation, demand an audience familiar with, and accepting of, the generic and stylistic conventions, as well as the cultural background, that inform the film. The experience of film requires at least some level of engagement, and some films demand rapt attention.

Films call for interpretation, and a third critical question posed by the film experience is how it is to be interpreted, whether a given understanding is adequate. Here, we might say, it is the audience itself being assessed. Failure to make sense of a movie often leads an audience to blame its makers – to consider them either pretentious or incompetent – and they may be right to do so, but whether in any case they are right is an issue posed by the experience. Note that this question, like the other two, isn't something audience members answer on their own. Each comes to the film with a set of assumptions drawn from their history and upbringing and culture, aware to some degree of the likely and actual reactions of others. Each knows he or she is answerable to these others, if just in the sense that he'll solicit their takes when he doesn't know what to make of something, or she'll defend her approach if others disagree. If the first question is that of the reality implied by or depicted in the film, and the second question is whether the experience of the film is worth having, this third question asks whether and how we can know it or make sense of it.

Making sense of experience more broadly takes place in a social context, where we have a shared language and cultural background and a world in common, but nevertheless see things differently due to differing perspectives or interests. Plato captures this in his allegory by having the prisoners argue over what they see in the shadow play before them. They see the same shadows, but connect the dots differently, and give them differing assessments based on their bearing on what matters to them. They disagree because their arguments are not, strictly, about what they see, but how they see it. Strictly speaking, we never argue over facts. We disagree about what the facts are and why they matter, and consider our opinions to be factual. In disputes over opinions, the best we can ever get is consensus, when several agree to see things the same way. This is true of our experience of cinema too. As long as we remain at the level of opinion, the question who is right becomes a question of who is more convincing, who can more effectively silence critics. To move beyond consensus, we need to change the subject. On the one hand, we can disagree productively about the facts only if we share standards for their interpretation. If, to take an easy example, someone were to claim that *Singin' in the Rain* was a terrible movie because in real life people don't break out into song and dance, it would betray a serious misunderstanding that could be cleared up by explaining, and perhaps also exploring, the idea of a musical. He might still say: "then I don't like musicals," but could no longer claim it was a bad film for being one – and could hardly claim it was a bad musical. In this case it would be obvious the claim was about him and his preferences (and his lack of discernment) and had nothing to do with cinema or with this particular film. To go further, confusions regarding cinema result from failure to distinguish clearly, as the allegory of the cave encourages us here, between audience, apparatus, moving image, and meanings. What is there on screen should be distinguished from how it affects or is interpreted by audiences; techniques (such as "pulling focus" or "panning" or "voiceover") should be distinguished from the significances they make visible and audible, the varied meanings they communicate.

On the other hand, even conceptual clarity is insufficient to eliminate all debates, and not all disagreements over standards can be resolved by making distinctions and defining terms. Different interests will still result in differing interpretations and assessments. While clarifying terms and paying attention to detail can resolve some interpretive differences, there are almost always a variety of informed approaches that remain. Here changing the subject means turning the focus away from finding a single, correct interpretation, and asking, instead, what each interpretation allows us to see, what questions it holds open and what questions it resolves. The best cinematic works can sustain multiple analyses, generating conversations about the world we inhabit, how we know it, and what really matters. The best cinematic works open up new horizons, new ways of seeing and new ways of thinking.

Beyond questions of interpretation, films enable audiences to inhabit, as it were, a variety of perspectives. Where perspectives differ or come into conflict, viewers are in a position to consider the adequacy of the various perspectives. Film reminds us, in fact, that what we encounter in the world is always from some perspective, and that not everything can be seen from any one point of view. Films naturally illustrate the power of skepticism, insofar as they can encourage audiences to interpret realities they depict from a point of view that can later be shown to be inadequate or problematic. Alex, for example, in *A Clockwork Orange*, may initially seem to be a reliable narrator, but his take on his own story is increasingly doubtful as the film reaches its finale.

Illuminating shadows (aesthetics)

Cinema, like any art and like life, is dynamic; it grows, always giving birth to new approaches, new forms, new ways of communicating, new ways of getting us closer to or creatively complicating the realities it depicts. Of course there is no shortage of derivative cinema, but there are always innovators from across the globe who manage to tell new stories in new ways. As celebrated film critic and theorist André Bazin argued, the guiding ideals of cinema preceded the technological innovations that realized it, and new techniques have only served to fulfill and amplify its initial promise of preserving for repeated contemplation realities in time. "In short," he argued, "cinema has not yet been invented!" Each new work of cinema, at least, has the potential to transform the senses according to which film experience is understood, and to challenge established answers to the kinds of questions cinema shares with philosophy. That cinema is alive like life is not to say that the concepts and questions of cinema – what we've compared here with the light in Plato's cave – are themselves unstable. To think change, to think what is different, requires a conception of identity against which the different appears. As noted already, the prisoners in Plato's cave can only make sense of the shadow play before them because they can compare what they see one moment with what arises next; they can discern something of the shape of a given shadow, and can say of each whether they consider it the same or different than another in some respect or other. They may be wrong about any particular identification or distinction, and they are confused about the ultimate reference of their notions, but their claims are not completely meaningless because they share a language and employ at least some common concepts.

Likewise, audiences of cinema operate with at least some conception of the cinematic experience, and some history of personal encounters with particular films. What is novel in cinema can only appear against the backdrop of audience expectations informed already by the history of established developments. To even count as cinema, an event must be capable of being grasped as such, which requires, as we've seen, at least a conception of film, of an audience, of some screening or projection apparatus. A number of other conceptions seem relevant, too – and we've seen how they function in the context of *A Clockwork Orange* – such as that of a moving image and of the cinematic frame, of perspective, of action, of character, of narrative, and more. A truly novel cinematic achievement, one without any precedent whatsoever, could only appear as something altogether different than cinema. The novelty of cinema is, like the novelty of history or of self-development, the novelty of that which defines and creates itself by relating itself to itself and opposing itself to itself. In the case of cinema, each new work that is not merely derivative comes to define cinema by simultaneously drawing upon audience expectations and subverting them, responding to extra-cinematic realities and imaginary constructions and transforming them in their depiction.

A final critical question the cinematic experience poses is that of artistic merit, whether a film works aesthetically, whether it offers something to be explored, independently of whether it feels right or real. Aesthetics can be construed narrowly, focusing on purely sensible qualities of the film, as when we think of how pretty are the visuals, or how formally precise the editing. When audiences walk away from a film saying things like "It was gorgeous to look at, but didn't make any sense" or "the camera work was unique but the story was weak" they are claiming it succeeded artistically on at least one level, but failed to win conviction, and thereby failed to work. When critics describe a film as fun but utterly forgettable, they are likely suggesting it works as entertainment, but fails as art. While such assessments can be quite subjective, in general a film that fails to win conviction fails as a film, however impeccable its artistic credentials. In a broader sense of aesthetic worth, however, when the question is whether the work enables one to see the world anew, in ways that reveal meanings hitherto unsuspected, the sensible properties of the film and the technical qualities of the work are inseparable from the question of what they make comprehensible. The critical questions outlined here – questions of reality, interpretation, of moral and aesthetic worth – are all in fact interconnected. Whether a film wins conviction, feels real, and whether it is judged aesthetically satisfying, depends on how it is experienced and understood, on what it allows to be grasped, on what it reveals and makes possible.

The notion that films can go beyond mere depiction of situations in order to reveal or illuminate the way things are and ought to be can be clarified somewhat by recalling the image of the divided line, which Socrates describes directly prior to his account of the cave, and employs afterwards to explain the allegory. In his account of the divided line, Socrates divides visible realities into images, grasped by way of imagination, and objects, that we perceive. He divides the intelligible realities into postulates or standards regarding how things are and ought to be, and the principles that enable us to revise those postulates and make sense of how they hang together. The divided line is a ladder, which begins with the apprehension of imagery and ends with insight into principles. Art, as we've seen, belongs to the realm of images, of shadows. The artwork is no work at all and doesn't work at all except as it delivers a sensible appearance. Still, the best works work like Socrates' imagery, his allegory of the cave, for example: they depict scenarios that push audiences to feel and think and see otherwise than they're used to, and in doing so, potentially at least, they push them upwards on the ladder.

Our knowledge of what is visible comes first from how things look to us. Mere appearances correspond to shadows in Plato's cave, and are misunderstood as long as we fail to grasp the realities giving rise to them. I might catch a glimpse in the distance of a friend from the side. Seeing his profile far away I see my friend. Yet if I fail to recognize him, or if I do but fail to see there's more to him than just how he happens to have appeared to me, I can't really know him. I have only opinions, unwarranted beliefs, impressions rooted in appearances. Even if I distinguish between him and his appearance, the best I can make are fallible judgments, attributing to him various traits hypothetically, some inconsistent with one another, based on experience and hearsay. According to Socrates, this is all we ever have until we actively interrogate the way things seem to us, and begin critically to assess the standards we employ in making sense of this or that appearance.

To understand a thing, anything at all, according to Plato, is to grasp what it is trying to be, what it exists to achieve – as we make sense of couches only when we know what a couch is supposed to be. To see what it is striving toward is to grasp its form or idea, the standard by which it is measured and grasped. The investigation of ideas or standards takes place through analysis and dialogue, as we propose what we take to be the common roots of a range of appearances, and come to see more precisely what our ideas entail and whether they are consistent. The investigation, throughout, presumes there's a way to make sense of conflicted and contradictory appearances; we make distinctions and refine the standards we employ in making sense of things because we grasp that they must make sense as a whole, that our standards must be consistent. To sort out the standards in terms of which the world makes sense as a whole requires a grasp or intimation, implicit at first but gradually more clear, of a standard for standards, an ideal.

Core ideals in Plato's work include ideas of being, knowledge, justice, and beauty, but the highest ideal, for Plato, that unifies the rest, is the idea of the Good. "The Good" in Plato's metaphysics has been thought to mean many things, but metaphorically for Plato in the *Republic* it functions as an intelligible light, a standard of standards, whose presence to us allows us to make sense of and sort out standards and ideas, in much the same way as the visible light of the sun allows us to view and differentiate the many visible things. To sort out the way things are, how to know them, how to be, and how to see the beauty in things, demands we consider not just what each thing strives to be, but what they altogether aim for and make possible. To consider reality in light of the Good is to ask not only how things are but also how they ought to be and could be.

It is, on Socrates' account, the intervention of philosophy that turns his cave dwellers toward the light, away from mere opinions regarding appearances and toward critical reflection on the ideas that inform them. Such reflections proceed by posing questions, making distinctions, exploring their implications, and revising conceptions in light of what is discovered. At the core of any such discussions are ideals, notions of what are the basic or ultimate terms whose understanding the discussion promotes. Because these ideals – of reality, knowledge, justice, and beauty – are both presupposed at the beginning of philosophical inquiry and clarified in its course, we might suppose the way ideals exist for us is by provoking live questions rather than providing settled answers. Questions about ways things are, for example, both presuppose and work toward an understanding of what it is to be, an idea of being, or of what it means to say of anything it is real. The ideal of being exists as the question "what is being?" – a question whose focused pursuit in wonder has traditionally been called metaphysics. When we compare competing assertions or interpretations, and ask which is true, which counts as knowledge, we are working from an assumption that we in some sense know what it is to know, and in fact serve to clarify the ideal of knowledge in the process. The ideal of knowledge exists as the question "what is knowledge?," the systematic inquiry into which is epistemology. The question how best to act in a given circumstance begs the question of what are standards for action, what it means to do right or be just. The ideal of justice or right action exists in us as the question "how should I act?" or "how should one be?" – a question that can be expanded into the domain of inquiry known as ethics. Assessments of artworks, and our capacity in general for finding some experiences compelling for their aesthetic qualities, suppose standards for aesthetic appreciation, such as the notion of beauty. The ideal of beauty exists for us as the pursuit of beauty and as the question "what is beauty?"; and since art is often understood as the creation of beautiful works, the question is often linked with "what is art?" Both inquiries, when they go beyond unfocused musings, form the domain of aesthetics.

None of these inquiries, into being, knowledge, ethics, and beauty, can ever be conclusively settled in such a way as to efface the basic questions at their heart. Being becomes, knowledge expands, ethics must act, and beauty creates, and so the inquiry into each of these is always openended. That is not the same as claiming it is always inconclusive or its answers are arbitrary. We learn a great deal along the way, but no one gets to say the last word. It is a rich and varied historical conversation, which sometimes reaches certain dead ends, but there are always those who manage to loop back and pick up on more productive threads. The conversation only becomes richer when it expands its reach to discover unexpected challenges and draw upon novel sources of insight.

Films offer philosophical illumination, they push us up the ladder, when they encourage audiences to explore basic questions like these, and when they challenge the usual responses. Films, on occasion, and sometimes with a bit of prodding, manage to lead spectators up the divided line, out of the cave and back again to consider the world differently. Thinking carefully about film, and along with such films, demands engagement with such questions, in conversation with philosophy. Whereas Plato's prisoners require the assistance of the philosopher even to initiate the inquiry, we've seen that the experience of cinema also solicits a critical awareness of related basic questions on the part of its audience. Once again, the encounter with the image solicits a comparison with the real, since we engage fully in the experience only insofar as it wins our conviction. The experience itself demands interpretation, and given it is something we often do with others, our ways of making sense provoke comparisons with alternatives. As something we do, watching movies poses the question whether we ought to. In telling stories about things people do, and sometimes seeming to side with one character or another, films invoke our appraisal of their apparent sympathies. What is more, because it is artificial, the cinematic experience at the same time encourages reflection on its qualities as craft and its aesthetic dimension. Of course these questions, provoked naturally as a result of watching even ordinary movies, rarely push us further than common sense and prejudice for their response. The critical question of reality usually amounts to no more than asking whether characters act as we expect and whether the plot is plausible. We take our interpretations of films for granted, and when we don't know how to make sense of them we assume they don't make sense. The question of ethics rarely goes further than to wonder whether a movie was a waste of time, or whether its content was offensive. Aesthetics reduces to a question of preference: did you like it or you didn't you?

Films push further when they manage to make us uneasy with the easy answers. The suggestion that films can be philosophical or, as is sometimes said, they "do philosophy," shouldn't be misunderstood to mean the images themselves think, and doesn't even need to mean the filmmakers are themselves philosophers. It is just to say that some films, whether by accident or design, provoke thoughts in an audience prepared to take them seriously. They pose philosophical questions and offer avenues for their response, and often offer reasons why the obvious answers are insufficient. All films, and film as such, to a greater or lesser degree, pose philosophical questions, whether explicitly or not, so that all film criticism has the potential to move in directions that have bearing upon and can enter into conversation with philosophy. Because this is so, we should expect that certain films, like *A Clockwork Orange*, where those involved in their creation have clearly thought carefully about the workings of the medium, will exhibit an intensified focus on one or more of the themes that cinema invokes naturally.

Late in life, Plato insisted he'd never written down his most important philosophical teachings, not because he was unwilling to share them, but because they can't be written down, except by way of indications to be followed up by those few listeners able and willing to find out for themselves. Instead of treatises he wrote dialogues, depicting conversations that were, usually, exciting and illuminating but inconclusive and incomplete. One might consider that, by themselves at least, his dialogues don't "do philosophy" except insofar as they provoke readers to carry on the conversations they depict, in ways that are informed and shaped by the many hints and provocations their careful readings have spelled out. Philosophy is vital and real only as conversation, and any given work of philosophy cannot and should not be the last word but only ever a beginning, a stimulus to analysis, critique, and dialogue. To say that films – in their rich interplay of shadows and light, silence and sound, word and image – are or can be philosophical, or that they are able to "do philosophy," is just to say that all of them can and ought to provoke some philosophical thinking, and some of them, at least, provoke questions about which they have something to say, but that their only way of saying it is to evoke considerations in the thinking of their attentive and critical audience. This book was written in the hopes of encouraging just such critical attention and in anticipation of the many rich conversations about cinema and about life to follow.

Suggested films

Readers interested in examining more films along the lines of the approach developed in this book may wish to consider those listed here. The first four, in their style and in their storytelling, draw upon and evoke thoughts regarding some of the classic themes of philosophy. The last of these and the rest suggest reflection on themes investigated in the present text: Plato's cave and cinema, voyeurism and violence, and the complexities of perspective.

Metaphysics – on reality and representation

Vertigo, *directed by Alfred Hitchcock, 1958*

A former detective with a fear of heights falls in love with the woman he is recruited to spy on. Unable to save her when she leaps to her death, he is rescued from depression when he finds another woman who looks just like his lost lover and attempts to remake her in the image of the original. The film troubles the relation between image and original, appearance and reality, performance and actor.

Aesthetics – on art's revelatory capacities

City Lights, *directed by Charlie Chaplin, 1931*

A bum meets a millionaire who embraces him as his best friend – but only when he's drunk. He falls in love with a blind woman, and is thrown in jail for his efforts to help her regain her sight. An indelible image at the end of the film highlights what it is truly to see eye to eye, and how societal divisions make it next to impossible.

Ethics – on honesty and responsibility

sex, lies and videotape, *directed by Steven Soderbergh, 1989*

The sudden visit by an old friend exposes the lies preserving a marriage intact. The film examines the ethics of the camera, as well as the connection between honesty and taking responsibility for the impact of our activity.

Epistemology – on perspective and knowledge

Rashomon, *directed by Akira Kurosawa, 1950*

In feudal Japan, a woman is raped, her husband, a samurai, murdered. Through a series of contradictory flashbacks, the film highlights the elusive nature of knowledge.

Images of Plato's cave

The Conformist, *directed by Bernardo Bertolucci, 1970*

A young Italian fascist is assigned to kill his former philosophy professor. During a pivotal scene, he recalls a lecture on the allegory of the cave in a darkened room, and the film throughout explores the societal and political pressures to conform, in opposition to the liberating power of thinking for oneself.

The Matrix, *directed by Andy and Larry (now Lana)* *Wachowski, 1999*

A computer hacker with an interest in conspiracies discovers the conspiracy is real and calls into question everything we think we know. The technological contrast between the real and the virtual, in this film, stands in for the distinction between the world we take for granted and the truth that it conceals.

Voyeurism and violence on film

Peeping Tom, *directed by Michael Powell, 1960*

A young man, whose emotional responses had been the subject of his father's scientific research, is now obsessed with capturing on film the frightened reactions of the women he obsesses over and pursues.

Blow Out, *directed by Brian De Palma, 1981*

A sound artist working on an exploitation film about a voyeur serial killer goes in search of the "perfect scream" and records evidence of a political killing instead. In his frantic search for the truth he recruits and falls in love with an unwitting accomplice to the crime.

Strange Days, *directed by Kathryn Bigelow, 1995*

In a near-apocalyptic Los Angeles, an ex-cop is now a hustler of illicit virtual reality clips, which allow the viewer to tap into the actual immersive experience of another person's life. He rethinks the legitimacy of his profession when he acquires a clip of a woman's brutal rape and murder from the perspective of the killer, but he may know too much to walk away alive. Issues of race, gender, politics, media ethics, and social justice intersect in this intense cyber-thriller.

Suggested readings (including all readings referred to in the text)

On Plato and the *Republic*

Blackburn, Simon. *Plato's Republic: A Biography*. New York: Grove Press, 2008.

Plato. *The Republic of Plato*, trans. Allan Bloom. New York: Basic Books, 1991.

——*The Symposium*, trans. Avi Sharon. Newburyport, MA: Focus Publishing, 1997.

——*The Apology of Socrates* in *Five Dialogues*, trans. G.M.A. Grube, rev. John M. Cooper. Indianapolis: Hackett Publishing Co., 2002.

Sallis, John. *Being and Logos: Reading the Platonic Dialogues*. Bloomington: Indiana University Press, 1996.

On Kubrick and *A Clockwork Orange*

Abrams, Jerold. *The Philosophy of Stanley Kubrick (The Philosophy of Popular Culture)*. Lexington: University Press of Kentucky, 2009.

Burgess, Anthony. *A Clockwork Orange (Norton Critical Edition)*. New York: W.W. Norton & Co., 2010.

Ciment, Michel. *Kubrick*. New York: Faber & Faber, 2001.

Krämer, Peter. *A Clockwork Orange (Controversies)*. New York: Palgrave Macmillan, 2011.

Naremore, James. *On Kubrick*. London: British Film Institute, 2008.

Shaw, Dan. "Freedom and Determinism in *A Clockwork Orange*," in *Morality and the Movies*. New York: Continuum Books, 2012, pp. 75–87.

On violence and pornography and the impact of media on society

Horeck, Tanya. *Public Rape: Representing Violation in Fiction and Film*. New York: Routledge, 2004.

Hurley, Susan. "Imitation, Media Violence and Freedom of Speech." *Philosophical Studies*, 117: 165–218, 2004.

Postman, Neil. *Amusing Ourselves to Death: Public Discourse in the Age of Show Business*. New York: Penguin Books, 2005.

Classics of aesthetics and film theory

Arnheim, Rudolf. *Film as Art*. Berkeley: University of California Press, 2006.

Baudry, Jean-Louis, "The Apparatus: Metapsychological Approaches to the Impression of Reality in Cinema," in *Film Theory and Criticism*, ed. Leo Braudy & Marshall Cohen. New York: Oxford University Press, 2009, pp. 171–88.

Bazin, André. *What is Cinema?*, 2 volumes, trans. Hugh Grey. Berkeley: University of California Press, 1967 and 1971.

Heidegger, Martin. "The Origin of the Work of Art," in *Basic Writings*, ed. David Farrell Krell. San Francisco: Harper Perennial, 1993, pp. 139–212.

Krakauer, Siegfried. *Theory of Film: The Redemption of Physical Reality*. New York: Oxford University Press, 1960.

Mulvey, Laura. "Visual Pleasure and Narrative Cinema," in *Film Theory and Criticism*, ed. Leo Braudy & Marshall Cohen. New York: Oxford University Press, 2009, pp. 711–22.

Münsterberg, Hugo. *Hugo Münsterberg on Film: The Photoplay: A Psychological Study and Other Writings*. New York: Routledge, 2001.

Perkins, V.F. *Film as Film: Understanding and Judging Movies*. New York: De Capo Press, 1993.

Philosophy through film (film as illustration and example)

Falzon, Christopher. *Philosophy Goes to the Movies*. New York: Routledge, 2007.

Litch, Mary. *Philosophy Through Film*. New York: Routledge, 2010.

Wartenberg, Thomas E. *Thinking On Screen: Film as Philosophy*. New York: Routledge, 2007.

The philosophy of film (film as subject matter for philosophical analysis)

Carroll, Nöel. *The Philosophy of Motion Pictures*. Malden, MA: Blackwell, 2008.

Plantinga, Carl & Smith, Greg, eds. *Passionate Views: Film, Cognition, and Emotion*. Baltimore, MD: John Hopkins University Press, 1999.

Thomson-Jones, Kathryn. *Aesthetics and Film*. New York: Continuum, 2008.

Film-philosophy (film as philosophy)

Carel, Havi, and Greg Tuck. *New Takes in Film-Philosophy*. New York: Palgrave Macmillan, 2011.

Cavell, Stanley. *The World Viewed: Reflections on the Ontology of Film*. Cambridge, MA: Harvard University Press, 1979.

——*Pursuits of Happiness: The Hollywood Comedy of Remarriage*. Cambridge, MA: Harvard University Press, 1984.

——*Contesting Tears: The Hollywood Melodrama of the Unknown Woman*. Chicago: University of Chicago Press, 1996.

Deleuze, Gilles. *Cinema 1 & 2*, trans. Hugh Tomlinson and Barbara Habberjam. Minneapolis: University of Minnesota Press, 1986 and 1989.

Mulhall, Stephen. *On Film*. New York: Routledge, 2008.

Sinnerbrink, Robert. *New Philosophies of Film: Thinking Images*. New York: Continuum, 2011.

Smith, Murray, and Thomas E. Wartenberg. *Thinking Through Cinema: Film as Philosophy*. Malden, MA: Blackwell, 2006.

Glossary of artists and thinkers, terms and concepts

What follows is a brief description of significant artists and thinkers, as well as key terms, from philosophy and film studies, that are either discussed or referred to indirectly within these pages. A reader's familiarity with these is not presumed, beyond how they are outlined in the text. Notably, the text deliberately avoids use of the technical terminology drawn from film production and film studies in order to describe a range of camera shots and techniques. The aim there is, rather, to focus on how the results are experienced by audiences, regardless of their background in the jargon of film analysis. The text also aims to avoid philosophical jargon, as well as the caricatures of philosophical positions that freshmen in philosophy classes sometimes memorize in lieu of themselves thinking through the things themselves the terminology is meant to signal. It is, nevertheless, hoped that a basic familiarity with some of this terminology will assist readers inspired by this text to go further in film studies or philosophy – or the philosophy of film or film-philosophy! – to appreciate and be conversant in some of the broader issues and debates that helped shape the thinking expressed therein.

Aesthetics – one of the core traditional areas of philosophical inquiry, aesthetics is concerned with the nature of art, and with concepts such as beauty. See also **Epistemology, Metaphysics,** and **Ethics.**

Apparatus Theory – a dominant approach within cinema studies of the 1970s; theorists who were influenced by Marxist film theory, psychoanalysis, and semiotics considered the impact of the institution of cinema as such on audiences. They considered that the "apparatus" of cinema – which includes the technological and industrial mechanisms whereby films are produced and distributed, marketed and projected for audience consumption – had an effect upon audiences that was independent of the content of this or that film. In this book, the "cinema apparatus" is identified as just one of three critical factors having bearing upon the significance and impact of cinema, which includes also the personal and societal background of the audiences, what they bring with them to the encounter, and the style and content of motion pictures themselves.

Aristotle (384–322 BC) – Plato's most famous student, who is often considered to have disagreed with his teacher regarding universals, or forms, which he considered to be observable and immanent in the things themselves around us, rather than existing in an abstract and timeless realm beyond (see **Plato's Theory of the Forms**). He wrote on an astonishing range of subjects – from logic to poetry, politics, and metaphysics, psychology to biology – but his most celebrated and influential work is likely the *Nicomachean Ethics*, in which he urged among other things that part of doing the right thing is training one's feelings and dispositions to want it.

Arnheim, Rudolf (1904–2007) – a German-born author, psychologist, art critic, and aesthetician whose most influential work on cinema (*Film as Art* – see Suggested Readings) was written on the cusp of the transition from silents to sound films. He urged, against critics who saw it as a merely mechanical recording device, that film was a formidable and distinctive new art form.

Auteur Theory – formulated in the 1950s by critics writing for the French film journal *Cahiers du Cinema*, "auteur theory" holds that some films can profitably be considered in connection with the body of work of an "author," most often their director. Film is an intensely collaborative enterprise, with many contributors, but some filmmakers, such as Kubrick, do seem to have a distinctive style and set of concerns that show up consistently in all or most of their works.

Baudry, Jean-Louis – a French film theorist, writing in the 1970s, who made use of neo-Freudian and neo-Marxist theories to argue that cinema, by its very nature, tended to position the subject as passive in relation to reality, and hence to treat as given or inevitable, and hence unassailable, institutions such as global capitalism (see Suggested Readings). See **Apparatus Theory**.

Bazin, André (1918–58) – a highly influential French film critic and co-founder of the film magazine *Cahiers du Cinema*; well-known as an exponent of **Realism** in cinema, he was fascinated above all by those filmmakers whose works seemed more interested in the discovery of compelling, unexpected, or hidden realities than in the design of an experience that could manipulate the emotions of audiences towards a pre-established end (see *What is Cinema?* in Suggested Readings).

Being versus Becoming – in the prelude to his account of the allegory of the cave, Plato distinguishes between a visible realm of change or becoming, ruled over by the Sun, and an intelligible eternal realm of being.

Brakhage, Stan (1933–2003) – one of the most influential and important of American experimental filmmakers. Famous for painting directly on filmstrips and scratching negatives deliberately, his films challenge attempts to define film in terms of the representation of moving objects, given that watching his films can feel like a direct encounter with flux.

Burgess, Anthony (1917–93) – an English novelist, musician, and screenwriter, primarily famous for writing *A Clockwork Orange* (see Suggested Readings). His concluding chapter, in which Alex grows up, was omitted from the American edition, on which Stanley Kubrick based his film.

Cavell, Stanley (1926–present) holds that the popular appeal of cinema stems in part from its capacity to address and overcome some of the basic problems of philosophy, and to situate these problems within the context of everyday situations and ordinary lives. Hollywood romantic comedies and melodramas, for example, depict individuals in pursuit of self-knowledge, who struggle to define themselves on their own and in relation to others, where problems of knowledge can impact intimate relationships, and **skepticism** is far more than an academic concern. A major influence on the development of **film-philosophy**, he is the first major American philosopher to have made film a central theme throughout his work.

Classical Style – also known as classical "Hollywood" style, its aim is to make technique invisible in the service of encouraging audience's emotional investment in a story. See, by way of contrast, **Formalism** and **Realism**.

Close-up – usually defined as a tight framing on an actor's face, which allows audiences to witness her emotional state or reaction, the close-up shot can also be used to draw attention to a specific object or salient detail such as a gun in someone's pocket or the time on the face of a watch.

Coverage – an approach to shooting scenes in which a "master shot" containing all of the action is complemented by close-ups, medium and long shots of specific moments, allowing the editor to construct the scene in a seamless way. Filmmakers such as Kubrick often frown upon this approach, taking it to suggest a lack of artistic vision as to how the final scene should look and what it should mean going into it.

Deleuze, Gilles (1925–95) – among the most prolific and influential French philosophers of the twentieth century, Deleuze wrote on a number of subjects, and his original work aimed to provide an alternative to a metaphysics that treats either substances, or self-contained realities, or totalizing systems as the paradigm of reality. His was a philosophy of difference, of process, of event, and he conceived of the basic task of philosophy as the creation of concepts that enable new ways of thinking. He considered the arts, including cinema, as allies with philosophy in this process, and his two-volume book on cinema (see Suggested Readings) aims to trace a shift in the kind of thinking that cinema has given rise to, from a thinking that focuses on relative motion to a thinking exposed directly to images of time in its unfolding.

Determinism – the thesis that all events, including human activity, are determined with necessity for reasons independent of free will. Medieval philosophers speculated, for example, that God's knowledge – of past, present, and future – entailed that human beings could never do otherwise than in accordance with what they were predetermined to do. Modern philosophers have considered that laws of nature determine human activity. There is significant debate regarding whether determinism is compatible with or contradicts the possibility of free will.

Diegetic and Non-Diegetic Sound – diegetic sound is sound that occurs as part of the story world of the film, and that, presumably, the characters in the film can hear. The music playing from Alex's stereo as he sits in his room is an example of diegetic sound, as is the "Ode to Joy" that blasts in the final sequence from speakers brought into the hospital by the Minister's minions. Other musical bits in the film, such as the Rossini that plays as Alex and his droogs beat up Billy Boy's gang, are examples of non-diegetic sound, as they are presumably not playing as part of the story but only for us, the audience, to give a tone of light-hearted whimsy to the otherwise violent and chaotic scene.

Dolly Shot – a "dolly" is a mobile platform for a motion picture camera, which is usually mounted on tracks to deliver very steady camera movements. Dolly shots provide an alternative to the camera **Zoom**, and the result appears more natural because the camera is actually moving towards or away from the subject. Dolly shots can also be used to "track" movement of an object – as when the camera keeps a runner or a vehicle centered within the frame even as it travels.

Editing – the act of placing two motion picture shots or sequences together, one after another. Edits can aim to create the illusion of a continuous action taking place on screen, or they can interrupt that action, creating a chaotic feel, or jumping from one time to another or one place to another.

Empiricism – a philosophical school that holds knowledge to begin and end with the senses, considering reason to amount to little more than the capacity to generalize based on experiences. See **Rationalism**, by way of contrast.

Epistemology – one of the core traditional areas of philosophical inquiry, interested in the question what is knowledge and whether and how it can be acquired. **Rationalism, Empiricism,** and **Skepticism** are among the most enduring and influential approaches to epistemological issues. See also **Metaphysics, Ethics,** and **Aesthetics.**

Ethics – one of the core traditional areas of philosophical inquiry, focused on the questions how we should act, on the nature of right and wrong, and the meaning of the core concepts of morality. Prominent schools of ethical thought include utilitarianism, which holds that the right action is the one that brings the greatest benefit to the greatest number, and virtue ethics, which holds that to be moral is to cultivate a good character. See also **Aesthetics, Epistemology,** and **Metaphysics.**

Film as Illustration – films offer vivid examples of scenarios that can illustrate, challenge, or complicate philosophical positions. Films have often been used in the classroom to bring ideas to life – and a number of textbooks have appeared that aim to introduce philosophy through film. Practitioners of **Film-Philosophy** sometimes criticize this approach for treating films themselves and their issues as secondary to philosophical discourse and its traditional concerns, although Thomas Wartenberg (see Suggested Readings) has argued that providing examples for philosophical analysis can by itself be a valuable contribution to philosophy.

Film-Philosophy – an approach to thinking about film that treats it neither merely as an illustration of philosophical positions (see **Film as Illustration**) nor as an object for philosophical analysis, but as a rich source of autonomous thinking and provocation to thought, which in some instances can be considered to "do philosophy" and can at very least contribute to philosophical thought. American philosopher **Stanley Cavell** and French philosopher **Gilles Deleuze** are usually considered the pioneers of this approach, which has been taken up more recently by a number of thinkers working in the fields of philosophy and film studies.

Formalism – championed by early film critics who held that cinema is more than merely a device for recording actions, formalism is an approach to filmmaking that takes advantage of the resources of cinema – such as editing, camera movement, and framing – as stylistic devices or in order to comment upon the subjects displayed within the film. *A Clockwork Orange* can be considered a formalist film. See, by way of contrast, **Classical Style** and **Realism**.

Genre – films tend to be classified or grouped by readily identifiable elements or themes or story type, or by the anticipated audience they might appeal to, or by the fact they draw upon a set of characteristic concerns. Knowing the genre establishes, for an audience, a set of expectations as well as a willingness to suspend disbelief in certain elements (such as superheroes) that are central to the genre.

Greek Tragedy – a theatrical form prominent in Ancient Greece and Asia Minor, and central to the cultural and religious life of Athenians in the fifth century BC. Major tragedians include Aeschylus, Sophocles, and Euripides. Plato's student **Aristotle** held that tragedy was an imitation of the activity of great persons, whose outcomes were of great import to their communities, and that they both appealed to and helped to alleviate the impact of the emotions of pity and fear.

Handheld Shooting – light motion picture cameras designed primarily for journalistic purposes during World War II made it possible for filmmakers to "go out into the streets" and shoot with minimal crews. Handheld camera work was, for many audiences, synonymous with documentary-style realism, and recent "found footage" films such as *Blair Witch Project* and *Cloverfield* use handheld cameras to heighten the sense among audiences that what they are witnessing is real. Stanley Kubrick, who was always extremely concerned about precise camera work, nevertheless used handheld cameras selectively to great effect, in films like *Dr Strangelove*, *A Clockwork Orange*, and *Full Metal Jacket*. In the latter film he even added some unsteadiness to the usually smooth **Steadicam** shots, in order to achieve the look of authentic "newsreel" footage.

Homer (seventh or eighth century BC) – while very little is known about him, he was long considered to be the composer of the epic poems *The Odyssey* and *The Iliad*, which together played an enormous role in the shaping of Greek cultural life, and had an immeasurable impact on the subsequent development of Western literature and art.

Kubrick, Stanley (1928–99) – starting out as a photographer in New York City, Kubrick was an enthusiastic learner, who taught himself how to make movies. After making a few indie pictures on shoestring budgets, he was asked to direct the Hollywood epic *Spartacus*. He insisted, afterwards, on complete artistic control. His best-known films, covering a range of styles and subject matters, include *A Clockwork Orange*, *2001: A Space Odyssey*, *Barry Lyndon*, *The Shining*, and *Full Metal Jacket*.

Long Shot – a technical term in film studies and filmmaking that refers to a camera framing wide enough to include the entire body of a central figure on screen. Like the **Close-up** and the **Medium Shot** it is notable that its primary reference is to the human body, but of course a shot that could include a standing human figure but doesn't is also referred to as a long shot. A long shot is considered an establishing shot when its aim is to show audiences the setting in which subsequent interactions and activities will take place.

Medium Shot – a technical term in film studies and filmmaking, referring to a camera framing somewhere between a **Long Shot** and a **Close-up**, with the aim of being close enough that both the faces and the bodily gestures of the figures on screen can be seen, as well as some elements of their surroundings. The opening shot of *A Clockwork Orange* begins as a **Close-up**, then widens to a **Medium Shot**, and finally ends as a **Long Shot**.

Metaphysics – one of the core traditional areas of philosophical inquiry, focused on the nature of reality, what it means to be real or exist, whether there are different kinds of reality, and, if so, how they can relate to one another. See also **Aesthetics**, **Epistemology**, and **Ethics**.

Mise-en-scène – the significant arrangement of elements on the screen. This can include both the arrangement of what is in front of the camera – which involves blocking, staging, costuming, and set design – as well as the framing of shots and the movement of the camera – or cinematography. Early film theorists considered mise-en-scène and **Editing** to be the primary formal resources of cinema, the ways in which filmmakers could construct meaning artistically in ways that were unique to cinema.

Mulvey, Laura (1941–present) – a British film theorist, author of the enormously influential essay "Visual Pleasure in the Narrative Cinema" (see Suggested Readings), which not only helped establish Freudian analysis at the heart of film studies in the 1970s, but which remains of interest – and is relevant to a study of *A Clockwork Orange* – for its contention that cinema caters to a heterosexual male gaze. Classical film depicts women in such a way that they are seen as "to be looked at" – their depiction is geared towards the satisfaction of a pleasure in looking or "scopophilia" – while it depicts males, and especially the male protagonist, as "to be identi- fied with" or as the ones through whom the audience can vicariously experience the thrills of the picture.

Münsterberg, Hugo (1863–1916) – a celebrated and prolific German philosopher and psychologist who took an early interest in the workings of cinema. His book *The Photoplay* (see Suggested Read- ings) is widely considered to be the first significant work in film theory. He argued for the distinctiveness of cinema as an art form, and noted, for example, that certain techniques of cinema were able both to mirror and to evoke psychological processes.

Phenomenology – an approach to philosophy that sets aside traditional philosophical dilemmas and distinctions, and investigates the struc- tures of the world as it appears within actual lived experience. The approach is focused more upon clarifying the experiential meaning of events and institutions than upon formulating arguments. Asso- ciated in the twentieth century with thinkers such as Edmund Husserl, Martin Heidegger, and Maurice Merleau-Ponty, the approach has important precursors in the works of Georg Hegel and Søren Kierkegaard, and can even be seen at work in early philosophers such as Plato and Aristotle.

Philosophy of Film – usually thought of as a specialized topic within **Aesthetics**, the philosophy of film focuses on film as a distinctive art form that poses unique questions, such as how to define its differ- ence from other art forms, what it means to identify a film's author (see **Auteur Theory**), and whether there can be a film language. Although the philosophy of film overlaps in its subject matter with film theory, it developed in the late 1970s in part as a response to a growing dissatisfaction on the part of philosophers and other students of film with the dominance of Marxist, psychoanalytic, and semiotic approaches to film theory. Many involved in the philosophy of film are interested in linking their analyses to discoveries about how the brain works, and in particular to the cognitive sciences.

Plato (428–348 BC) – born into a prominent Athenian family, and showing great political promise, Plato was fascinated by the figure of **Socrates**, and arguably it was his teacher's execution by Athens that led him to leave politics aside in favor of education. Plato founded the Academy, which became a model for institutions of higher learning; he was **Aristotle**'s teacher and the author of a great many philosophical dialogues (see Suggested Readings), most of which feature **Socrates** as the leading discussant.

Plato's Theory of Forms – according to caricature accounts of his philosophy, Plato believed in a timeless realm of eternal essences (forms) that have always existed, and of which everyday objects are pale, imperfect copies. The reading in this text suggests that the timelessness of forms be considered akin to the openness of questions. The form of a couch, for example, would be what we glimpse when we take seriously the question "what is a couch" with the understanding that no specific couch invented yet exhausts the possibilities of what it is and can be.

POV Shot – a motion picture sequence designed to create the impression of depicting a single character's point of view, either simply to show audiences what he or she is seeing or in order to deliver a sense for how he or she sees the world. The handheld, chaotic shots from the rape scene inside the writer's house are not strictly suggestive of any character's specific point of view, and yet they appear designed to deliver a subjective sense of the confusion and disorientation that Mr and Mrs Alexander were feeling.

Rationalism – a philosophical school that holds reason to be the ultimate source of knowledge. **Plato** is often thought of as a rationalist, while his student **Aristotle** is considered to lean more towards empiricism. The most famous of modern rationalists is René Descartes ("I think, therefore I am"). See **Empiricism**.

Realism – film theorist **André Bazin** argued for the vitality and importance of a distinctive approach to filmmaking that made use of long takes, location settings, handheld cameras, and non-professional actors in order to create the impression that what took place on screen was not merely a spectacle but offered a window onto a reality unfolding in its own time and on its own terms. See, by way of contrast, **Classical Style** and **Formalism**.

Shot/Reverse-Shot – a very common sequence of shots designed to convey the impression of a perception or an interaction. A **Close-up** of someone looking in shock, for example, could follow a shot of a dead body, to convey the idea that she was witnessing the body. Conversations are often depicted in this way, when a shot over the shoulder of one person talking to another is followed by a shot over the shoulder of the other person looking at the first.

Skepticism – the philosophical position that knowledge is not possible. Socrates himself was often considered a skeptic, because he insisted that he knew nothing, except perhaps for the modest human knowledge of the limits of his claims. Ancient proponents of skepticism considered it a way of life, one that could alleviate the anxiety that comes from uncertainty. Modern skeptics, such as Hume, thought it was theoretically necessary to accept the limits of knowledge, even if practically it was impossible to live by doubting all.

Socrates (*c.* 469–399 BC) – what is known about Socrates comes from the writings of others, since he himself never wrote anything, but spent his time talking with a variety of people, encouraging them to consider the soundness of their ideas and values. He figures prominently in the dialogues of his most famous student, as well as in writings by the soldier and historian Xenophon and in Aristophanes's satirical comedy *The Clouds*.

Steadicam – a device used to stabilize a motion picture camera while allowing for a wide range of movements on the part of its operator. Stanley Kubrick was one of the first major filmmakers to use one, during the filming of *The Shining*.

Voiceover – a narrative device of cinema in which audiences hear the voice of one or more of the characters, or of a narrator, who are not shown to be speaking in the accompanying images. While it is sometimes used to fill audiences in on information that might be better displayed on screen, it is most effective when what is said in voiceover complements or serves as counterpoint to the images, as it does in *A Clockwork Orange*.

Zoom – a technique of cinema made possible by telephoto lenses, which can change their focal length in order to magnify what is seen on screen. Zooms allow for shots that move rapidly and smoothly from a **Close-up** to a **Long Shot**, for example, and vice versa. Contrast with **Dolly Shot**.

Appendix: Summary of Plato's *Republic*, book by book

Book I – As Socrates and Glaucon begin a long ascent homewards, to Athens, from the port where they'd witnessed a festival, they are stopped by Polemarchus and his friends, who insist that they visit him in his home and stick around for more festivities that evening. Socrates begins a conversation with Cephalus, the father of Polemarchus, who tells him that the great advantage of getting old is freedom from sexual desire, and that the great advantage of having money is the ability to pay off one's debts, so that one needn't fear being condemned as unjust in the afterlife. Thus begins a long conversation about the nature of justice, at first with Polemarchus, who considers justice to be a matter of giving what is owed: providing benefits to friends and harming one's enemies. Socrates convinces him it is never just to do harm to anyone, but then Thrasymachus attacks him, insisting that what we call justice only benefits the strong, and that the weak are just only out of fear. Socrates replies that unless the strong know what is good for them, they can hardly benefit from acting out of their perceived self-interest. Thrasymachus is forced to concede, reluctantly, that to live a good and happy life one needs to live well and be just.

Book II – Glaucon and his brother, Adeimantus, take up the argument where Thrasymachus left off. They tell Socrates they'd like to believe that the just are happy, but they fear that most people will act justly only out of concern for the consequences of being caught behaving badly. In order to clarify the nature of justice as it exists in the individual, Socrates proposes that they examine justice at the level of the city-state. They imagine a city being built up from scratch, in order to consider where injustice might emerge. If the city expands to much larger than a small village, whose villagers would be content to have only what is necessary, then the city will require a military or a guardian class, and these will require sustenance at a level possible only through a division of labor. They consider the qualities required for a guardian and determine that the first and most important task of their education is to determine the kinds of stories they should be told from a young age.

Book III – They discuss what kinds of content should not be included in the stories aimed at educating the guardians. They raise serious concerns regarding the impact of stories told by an imitator, who pretends to be the various characters in the stories he tells. They discuss the musical and physical educations of the guardians, and the need to tell a "noble lie" that will convince the citizens not to aspire to become members of a class to which their natural qualities are not suited.

Book IV – Justice in the city turns out to depend on each of the members of the city doing well what they are most suited for. Those driven above all by a sense of honor and duty are suited to service as guardians, and the best among them, who exhibit a philosophical nature and who care to know and be wise, will become leaders. Those driven by desires and a love of money are best qualified as workers and merchants and artisans. As this is justice in the city, so justice in the soul will turn out to be where insight and understanding rule over appetites and aspirations. When we pursue desires and honor only as appropriate and within measure, the soul is healthy and harmonious; when we are out of balance, we do damage to ourselves. So injustice turns out to be a kind of sickness in the soul.

Book V – While Socrates seems to think that their discussion has reached an end, some of those listening want to know more about the life of the guardians, who were said to share all things in common. They wanted to know whether this applied to their sexual life as well as their possessions. Socrates, with some apparent reluctance, suggests that men and women alike should train together as guardians, and that a greater unity among them would develop if they thought of each other as one large family, with children raised communally, rather than divided into various family units that might contend with one another. He suggests various measures the leaders might take to ensure the very best offspring from pairings between guardians, and to ensure against incest. He saves his more radical suggestion until the end, that the very best city should be led by philosophers, whose primary interest is in wisdom and who do not desire power for its own sake.

Book VI – Adeimantus worries that philosophers are too detached and out of touch to lead well, and Socrates argues that this only seems to be the case because very few pursue philosophy in the right way. To illuminate the nature of genuine philosophical understanding, Socrates introduces the image of the divided line and compares "the Good," which the philosophers seek, with the sun that illuminates all life on Earth.

Book VII – Socrates continues his account of the nature of philosophy in relation to everyday life by introducing the allegory of the cave. He then develops further an account of the proper education of philosophers, which goes from music and gymnastics, to mathematics, and then dialectic.

Book VIII – Socrates returns to the conclusions they'd developed regarding the best city, and examines how such a city might degenerate over time, resulting in other kinds of less than ideal but familiar types of city: from monarchy to oligarchy to democracy and then tyranny. Each of these types of city, he argues, results when the ideal of the previous one reaches its logical conclusion.

Book IX – The nature of the tyrant, and an account of how the tyrant might emerge in the context of a democracy, are the focus of this book. In order to clarify this nature, Socrates discusses the various pleasures that motivate us. The chapter concludes with a reiteration and expansion of the idea developed in Book IV that the happiest human being is the one who is just, who lives the life of the best city inwardly as well as outwardly.

Book X – Socrates returns to some of the concerns about poetry and imitative arts that dominated early discussions of the education of the guardians. He develops further an account of their effect on the soul of those who hear them. He concludes by recounting the myth of Er, a story of the afterlife in which it is suggested that souls choose their next lives based on an incomplete image of them, an image of the externals of those lives rather than an understanding of the kind of internal development that is necessary for true happiness.

Index